THE BODY

FOR BEGINNERS™

Dani Cavallaro

Illustrated by

Carline Vago

Orient Longman

ORIENT LONGMAN LIMITED

Registered Office
3-6-272 Himayatnagar, Hyderabad 500 029 (A.P), India

Other Offices
Bangalore/Bhopal/Bhubaneshwar/Calcutta/Chandigarh
Chennai/Ernakulam/Guwahati/Hyderabad/Jaipur
Lucknow/Mumbai/New Delhi/Patna

Book Design: Emma Byrne
Cover Design: Suzetta Bozzi

Published by arrangement with
Writers and Readers Limited
P O Box 29522
London N1 8 FB

First published in India by
Orient Longman Ltd 2001

ISBN 81 250 2024 1

Printed in India at
Novena Offset Printing Co.
Chennai 600 005

Published by
Orient Longman Ltd
160 Anna Salai
Chennai 600 002

THE BODY

FOR BEGINNERS®

BY DANI CAVALLARO

ILLUSTRATED BY CARLINE VAGO

contents

Why the Body?

The Body and Society

The Body and Philosophy

The Body in the Visual Field

The Body in Cyberculture

Conclusion: Incorporations

Why the body?

Outline

In recent years, the body has been radically rethought by both science and philosophy. We can no longer view the body as a natural object. The body is actually a cultural representation, constructed through various media, especially language. Societies produce ideals of the proper body in order to define their identities. Yet time and again, the body's boundaries turn out to be uncertain.

rethinking the body

Why is it that today the body is the focus of so much attention? How can we explain the current explosion of publications on the subject of the body, in both the popular media and in academic circles?

Maybe talking about the body is simply fashionable. Or perhaps, so much body-chatter is an effect of our anxieties about what the body is or is supposed to be.

In recent years, the body has been redefined by the claim that the physical form is not a natural reality, but a cultural concept: a means of encoding a society's values through its shape, size and ornamental attributes.

The body is produced by the meeting of physical drives and a society's supervision of those drives. A culture's body ideals speak volumes about how that culture perceives itself, or wishes to be perceived. They also help us understand how conventions can be perpetuated, or else challenged and reframed.

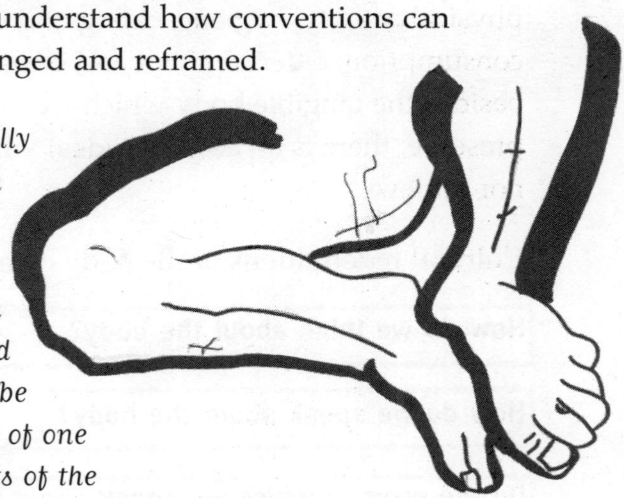

The body has also been materially restructured by science through practices such as genetic engineering and artificial insemination, and devices such as life-prolonging machines and artificial wombs. The body can be disassembled by plugging parts of one body into another. Various parts of the anatomy can be rebuilt through cosmetic surgery. Ultimately, the human organism may be replaced by automata which can perform quite efficiently many of the tasks once associated with the natural body.

Industrial and postindustrial societies have inserted into the social space replicas of the human body in the form of more and more complex tools, such as electronic systems of information and communication, which both complement and mirror human activities. But this is not to say that the meat and bones body has disappeared. In fact, societies go on developing intricate techniques of the body which vary according to race and gender.

They range from the weaning and rearing of small babies, through rites of initiation in adolescence, to the circumstances of adult life. They shape all everday experiences: sleep and waking, rest and physical activity, hygiene, eating and drinking, reproduction, consumption, entertainment and creativity. They also show that besides the tangible body which we are expected to care for and preserve, there is an aesthetic ideal which we might or might not achieve.

Cultural redefinitions of the body compel us to ask ourselves:

How do we think about the body?

How do we speak about the body?

Do the ways in which we speak about the body affect the ways in which we think about it?

the body and language

What is the body? What is a body? Is the body a substance, an idea, or a ***word?***

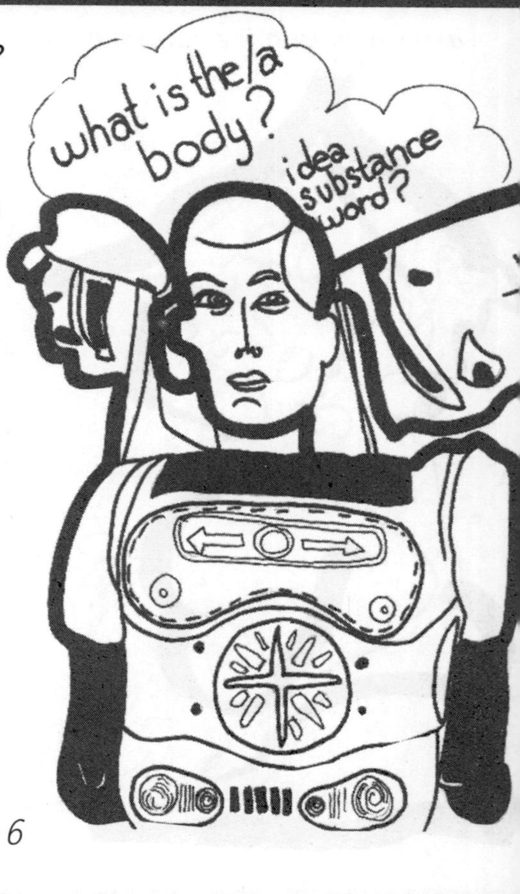

Many contemporary philosophers argue that there are no substances or ideas outside language. Substances and ideas are not realities which language reflects but rather **cultural categories** which language constructs.

The body is no exception. It, too, is primarily a product of language, **a representation**. It is only through language that the body gains meaning.

Language organizes the body according to the beliefs of a particular culture. This means that the human body is not a universal concept but rather a flexible idea, which can be **interpreted** in diverse ways, depending on time, place and context. If images can be made, they can also be unmade. There are many ideal images of the body which we are encouraged to take for granted, as if they were god-given. But once we realize that these images are constructed, it becomes possible to question them, to see them as **myths** rather than truths. Often, the **'ideal'** is only ideal for certain people, it only fuels limited interests.

How many bodies can we think of?

We **have** bodies, which suggests that the body can be treated as a property or possession. But we also **are** bodies, which suggests that the body is a state of being. The body can be thought of as **singular**, to describe an individual identity, or **collective**, to describe a corporate identity. The body is both **material**, as a physical organism, and **immaterial**, e.g. a body of beliefs, legends or myths.

Texts can be seen as bodies: they grow, change, develop or fall apart much as biological organisms do. Conversely, bodies can be seen as texts on which a person's history is written line by line.

The body can be used as a metaphor to describe the nation, its territory and its political structures and hierarchies: **the body politic**.

There are naked and clothed bodies; healthy and diseased bodies; diminished and muscular bodies; heroic bodies; sacrificial bodies; cannibalistic bodies; dead bodies; possessed bodies; part-bodies; supernatural bodies; heavenly bodies; geometric bodies... etc.

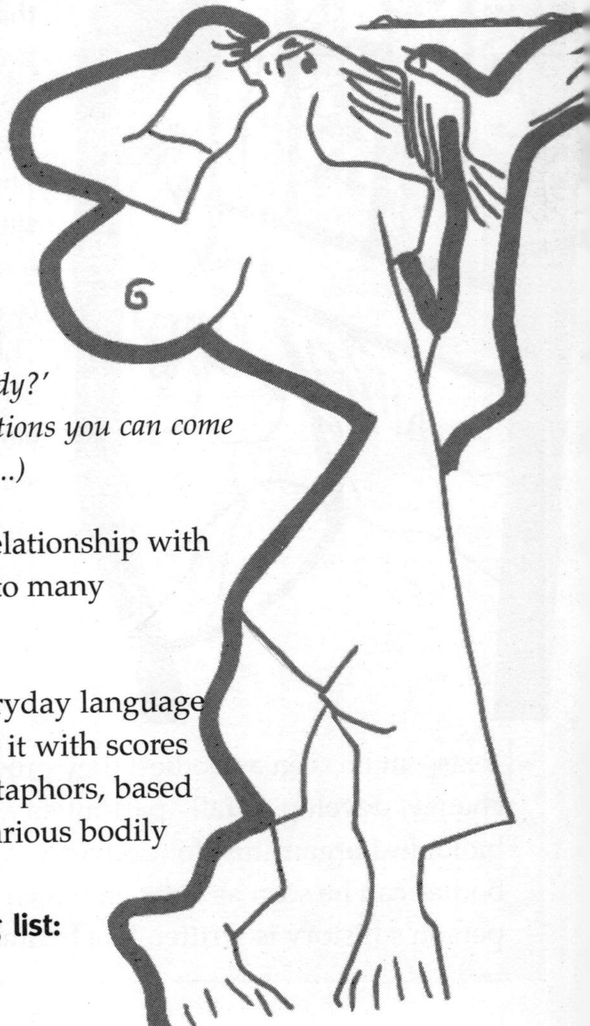

(This list is not exhaustive. When you have a few minutes to spare, try out a brainstorming exercise: sit down with a piece of paper and a pen, ask yourself 'what is the body?' and see how many different definitions you can come up with and put down in writing...)

The body, then, has a special relationship with language in that it lends itself to many possible interpretations.

But the body also inhabits everyday language in another sense, by supplying it with scores of idioms, expressions and metaphors, based on parts of the body and on various bodily functions.

For example, take the following list:

to swallow one's pride, to get something off one's chest, to feel it in the bones, to be spineless, to be limp-wristed, to be thick-skinned, to be an arsehole, to have guts/balls/spunk, to rack one's brains, to kick oneself, to bite one's tongue, to pull a face, to jump out of one's skin, to bleed someone dry, to hand it to someone, to bend someone's ear, to lend an ear, to turn a blind eye, to be nosy, to twist someone's arm, to cut off one's nose to spite one's face, to stand out like a sore thumb, to elbow someone out of the way, to shoulder a burden, to get one's finger out, to get stuffed, to wrap someone round one's little finger, to keep abreast of someone, to put one's finger on it, to stick one's foot in it,to lend a shoulder to cry on, to have one's nose out of joint, to be tongue-in-cheek...

The body doesn't just live in language. It also has its own languages.

Traditionally, we have been prompted to think about the body as a lumpish object which doesn't speak physically in any important ways. It only speaks significantly, we are told, when the *mind* propels it to say something.

Yet, the body does speak in many material ways. Body language tells us much about an individual's perception of her/himself, about emotions, feelings, and personality traits. The study of body language also gives us insights into ways in which people interrelate with one another - team together by adopting similar postures, gestures and mannerisms, for example, or separate themselves off from others by choosing personal, even idiosyncratic attitudes.

The body also speaks in many different ways through each of its senses. Western culture has traditionally regarded sight as the most important of the five senses, as a means to knowledge and control of ourselves and others. Although relatively neglected, however, the other senses have their own language systems, too. Several contemporary texts could be quoted to illustrate this.

Take Laura Esquivel's novel and film **Like Water for Chocolate,** for instance: this is essentially a tale about the language of taste, articulated through the detailed description of popular Mexican recipes and of their physical and emotional effects on those who prepare and consume them. Thus, although the young lovers Tita and Pedro are prevented from consummating their love due to familiar prohibitions, they can still express their feelings towards each other and communicate their passion to others through food.

Jane Campion's film ***The Piano****, as a further example, dramatizes the language of sound. Although the protagonist, Ada, is mute, she is still able to convey complex states of mind and feeling by playing her music, and to use the piano as a means of building important relationships.*

Italo Calvino's stories **The Name, the Nose; A King Listens;** and **Under the Jaguar Sun** use the languages of smell, hearing and taste respectively, to suggest ways in which the body may speak through its senses more successfully than through verbal language. We have the tale of a man who pursues the woman he loves guided only by her smell; the tale of a monarch who can only relate to his realm through the sounds which reach his isolated throne; and that of a couple who, no longer able to communicate either verbally or sexually, regain intimacy through the shared experience of eating.

Patrick Suskind's novel **Perfume** is devoted wholly to the language of smell. Smell is the most neglected of the senses because it is associated with basic bodily functions, primitive and savage behaviour, animal sexuality, poverty and disease. Smell disturbs us because it threatens our bodily boundaries: we constantly emanate and inhale odours in uncontrollable ways. By and large, we can choose what to touch or taste. Sights and sounds may impose themselves on us but do not penetrate us as literally as smells do. **Perfume** makes olfaction central to human existence.

Its protagonist, Grenouille, has no bodily odour of his own but spends his entire life classifying, inventing and refining powerful essences, to concoct a scent which will cause people to love him unreservedly. So powerful is the product of his experiments that the people who come into contact with it throw themselves into wild orgies. Ultimately, they want Grenouille's body so badly that they get hold of it and tear it apart.

boundaries

All cultures aim at building a sense of identity, and identity has a lot to do with how we perceive our own and other people's bodies. This may explain why different societies have regularly tried, through a variety of laws and rituals, to delimit the body: to erect clear **boundaries** around it.

Yet, the body's boundaries are difficult to trace. They are uncertain, for: how **can we confidently establish where the body 'begins' and where it 'ends'?**

There is no obvious way, for example, of separating the body's inside from its outside. Hair, nails, orifices, corporeal waste and secretions, and the skin itself, can be seen both as important parts of the body and as secondary appendices. The difficulty of demarcating the body's boundaries is complicated further by countless forms of bodily decoration - clothing, make-up, tattooing, piercing, body-painting, scarification.
Both cinema and literary fiction often dramatize the fear that the body's boundaries are unstable and can be breached in horrific ways. **Silence of the Lambs** offers a graphic representation of this idea.

Here, the body's boundaries are violated by recourse to one of the greatest taboos in western civilization: cannibalism. Hannibal Lecter literally eats the bodies of his victims and, in one case at least, turns the skin into a 'mask'. Buffalo Bill sews garments out of the skin of the women he fattens and then murders. The fragility of the natural body is gruesomely exposed as its physical attributes are turned into artifacts. Paradoxically, although the crimes presented in the story are overtly brutal, they are also made into sophisticated rituals: Lecter takes pride in announcing that he has eaten the liver of one of his victims with the accompaniment of a bottle of Chianti.

This suggests that there is nothing sacred about the body's boundaries and that even when these boundaries are destroyed in especially violent ways, the destruction can be made to appear a carefully 'staged' cultural act.

The body, in other words, is not a bounded whole, despite many a culture's efforts to make it appear to be so.

A body that is fluid and fragmented may sound like fun. If the body is not one fixed 'thing', but many possible 'bits' of things, the opportunities for play and experiment become virtually endless. Yet, the recognition that the body lacks wholeness has been, primarily, a source not of pleasure but of anxiety and fear.

Advertizing exploits this fear by constantly inviting us to think of ourselves as incomplete beings. Items as disparate as garments and accessories, jewellery and other ornaments, skin-rejuvenating cosmetics and tips for successful interior design, fabric and hair conditioners, fashionable kinds of food and drink, designer holidays and pets, to name but a few at random, are all presented as ways of rounding out the **lacking body.**

However, these items have no inherent value: they are continually displaced by other similar items in ongoing fashion cycles and recyclings. They become interchangeable with one another at all times. They cannot fulfil the lacking body in any lasting way: no sooner is an apparently complete body image achieved than hosts of so-called new, more fashionable items appear on the scene, to make that image look outmoded and in need of further reshaping.

In all societies, the feeling that the body is incomplete is conveyed through ritual, mythological and popular figures based on the idea of the part-body: a combination of the human and the non-human. The part-body may be partially human and partially animal, or partially biological and partially mechanical. Think of the werewolf, of the vampire, of Frankenstein's monster: these images are still very much with us today. That the vampire, for example, is still hugely popular is demonstrated by the success met by vampire narratives well after the publication of Stoker's **Dracula** (1897) - take Coppola's filmic remake of Stoker's story in 1992, or Anne Rice's bestselling **Vampire Chronicles** (1976-1995) and Tom Holland's **The Vampyre** (1996). The enduring attraction of the blood-drinker may have something to do with the fact that vampires, having once been human, are closer to us than other preternatural creatures, and are therefore more ambiguous and troubling.

From time immemorial, human beings have been telling stories about part-human and part-animal bodies, both in order to express the subliminal awareness that the body is not whole and to keep the fear of bodily incompleteness at bay. Mermaids, sirens, harpies, hydras, centaurs, satyrs, sphinxes, garudas, devils and angels are just a few examples of the many hybrid creatures that populate folklore and mythology throughout the world.

Hybrids take us back to a primitive, magical world which disregards conventional compartments. Identity is a phenomenon of endless transformation. The figure of the shaman, as conjuror of spirits, trickster and healer, able to transmute himself into powerful animal forces in the shadowy depths, epitomizes this world of continuous mutation. Both the hybrid body and the shaman's body emphasize that unity is an illusion by disrupting the boundaries between the human and the animal, the natural and the constructed, the physical and the non-physical. There is something chilling about this message. But there is also the promise of a world where we may not need to fear partial and contradictory identities, and may actually enjoy the idea of a continually disassembled and reassembled self.

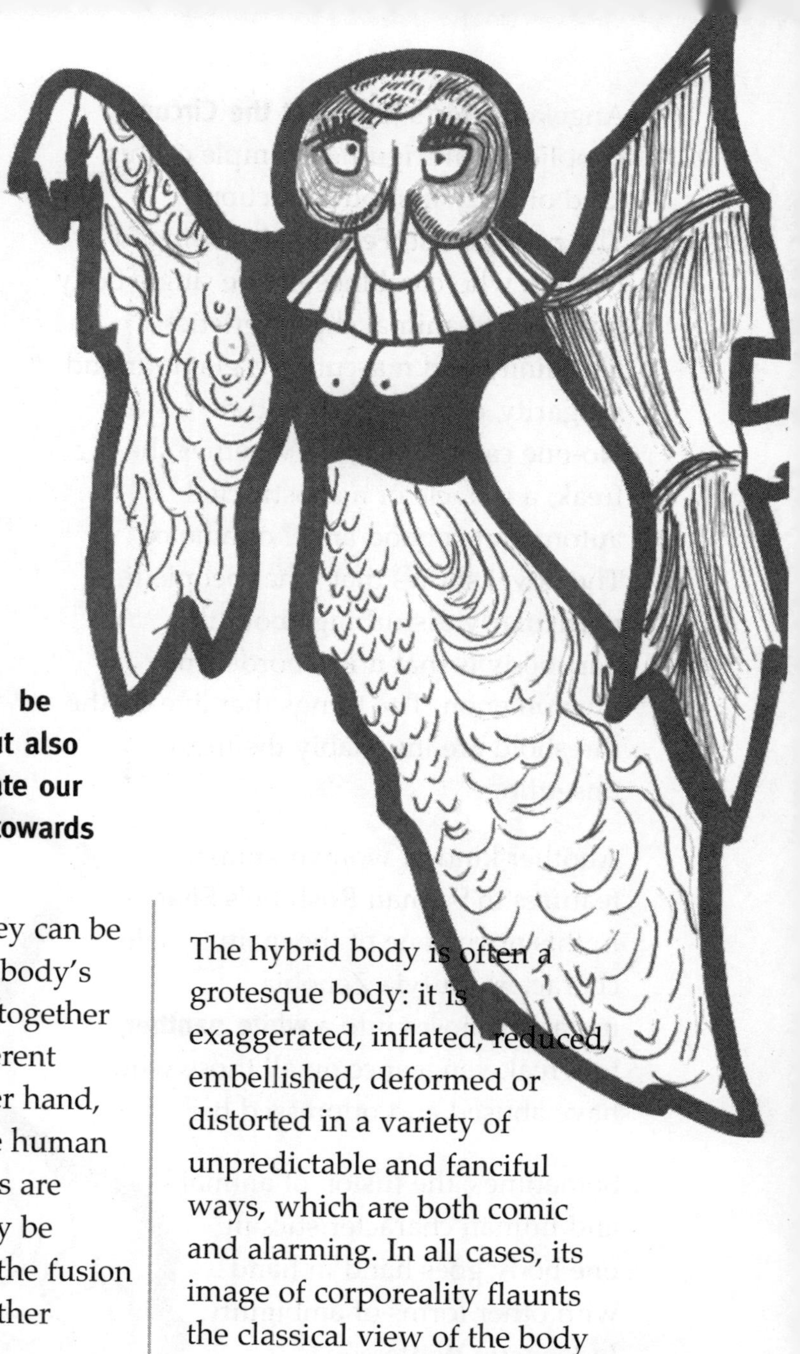

Hybrid bodies are ambiguous not only because they cannot be easily categorized but also because they incarnate our ambiguous feelings towards our own bodies.

On the one hand, they can be used to enhance the body's powers by bringing together the strengths of different animals. On the other hand, they suggest that the human body's own strengths are limited and may only be maximized through the fusion of the human with other natural forces. The permutations which give birth to a hybrid suggest that everything is interconnected in the natural world, and that the human body cannot aspire to a dominant position.

The hybrid body is often a grotesque body: it is exaggerated, inflated, reduced, embellished, deformed or distorted in a variety of unpredictable and fanciful ways, which are both comic and alarming. In all cases, its image of corporeality flaunts the classical view of the body as harmonious, balanced and ordered. What is most tantalizing about the hybrid, grotesque body is that it is often difficult to tell what is natural and what is artificial about its form.

Angela Carter's **Nights at the Circus** supplies an intriguing example of this kind of body in modern fiction. The protagonist, Fevvers, is a winged woman who combines in one single body human and animal characteristics, femininity and masculinity, glamour and vulgarity, enchantment and revulsion. No-one can tell for sure whether she is a freak, a miracle or a constructed automaton, a good angel or a hoax. The novel shows that what people find particularly disturbing about the part-body is that it is a borderline phenomenon. The things that live on the threshold are invariably the most unsettling.

Another kind of woman-animal features in Salman Rushdie's **Shame.** In this novel, one of the main female characters, Sufyia Zenobia, metamorphoses into a **white panther**, to wreak vengeance on all those who have abused and oppressed her.

Sometimes, the fusion of animal and human characteristics in one body goes hand in hand with other forms of ambiguity. In Jeanette Winterson's **The Passion,** for instance, the protagonist Villanelle has **webbed** feet, and is also a bisexual crossdresser with no regard for conventional distinctions between good and evil.

The body and society

Outline

Cultures express themselves through body images which pervade all aspects of everyday life. Understanding a culture means understanding its body images. Not all images enjoy the same status: some are commended, others are censored. At all times, the body is **disciplined** through various channels, such as the legal and educational systems, and controlled systematically by disciplines such as medicine. But no system or discipline can give a unified account of the body. There is no one scientific 'map' of the body universally applicable to all societies.

introduction

The body is, at one and the same time, part of nature, culture and society.

It is part of nature because it is associated with physical activity, sex and eroticism. And it is part of culture and society because it is associated with economic welfare, consumer culture, dietary practices, health and fitness.

Cultures rely heavily on the separation between **proper** bodies, to be glorified and imitated, and **improper** bodies, to be scorned and excluded. Controlling the body means controlling desire: not only **what** people desire but also **how** they desire it. We are told that certain objects are desirable, but we are also told that they can only be desired in certain places and at certain times.

The Protestant work ethics, for example, tells us that it is right to desire fun only after a spell of hard work. This yields a **split body:** thrifty and self-denying while it is producing, prodigal and self-indulgent while it is consuming. The **producer**-self and the **consumer**-self live together in a double-bind personality. This is characteristically illustrated by magazines which juxtapose pictures of luscious food and low-calorie regimes.

The ways in which we think about the body and represent it through various media are dictated by our historical circumstances. If we are particularly concerned with the fate of the body today, it is largely because we are anxious about the fate of a culture approaching the end of a millennium. The world around us shifts gears. And our bodies are compelled to do the same.

The end of the twentieth century and of the second millennium AD has witnessed some dramatic phenomena where the body is concerned: threats to the natural environment; the epidemic of AIDS and HIV; the increasing average age of many populations of northern Europe; the danger of chemical warfare; biotechnology's manipulation of the DNA.

The most apocalyptic thinkers believe that the body has reached **fatal extremes,** that we can only think about the body in terms of distortions and aberrations. The artificial or simulated body has become more real than the natural body. All physical movement has turned into breakneck speed. Ugliness has reached beyond itself into the realm of the monstrous. Sexuality has been inverted by porn.

eating bodies

Transformations in our body ideals are closely related to changing attitudes to food and diet. The ways in which human beings perceive food depend on the economic structures of their societies.

In the Middle Ages, it was quite normal for all social classes to alternate between feasting and fasting. Living conditions were precarious and insecure due to the high incidence of famines and to horrendous mortality rates. People fantasized about lands of amazing plenty, such as Cockaigne, and associated food availability with status. At the same time, sumptuary laws forbade lavish banquets as a form of excessive display and a possible cause of social unrest. The medieval body was torn between extremes and made emotionally volatile by its relation to food.

In the sixteenth and seventeenth centuries, the ability to stuff oneself and to show this off through physical bulk spelled out prosperity and power. Catherine de Medici, for example, was celebrated on account of her gargantuan appetite and frequent indigestion!

Gradually, a shift occurred from the ideal of quantity to that of quality.

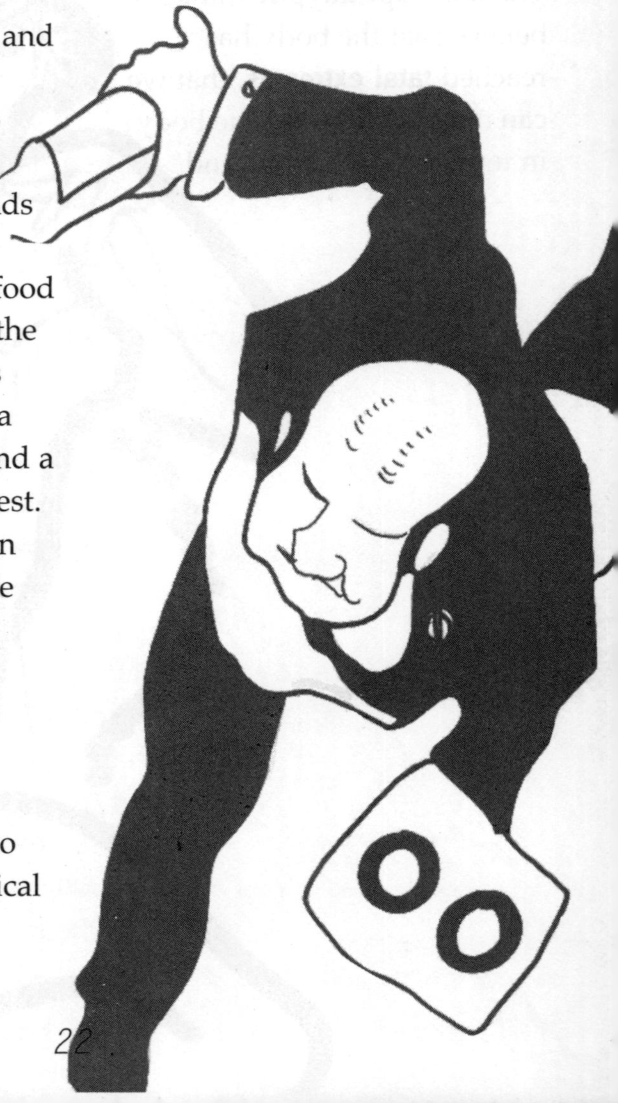

In the eighteenth century, as food supplies became more regular, reliable and varied, people became concerned with notions of good taste, sophistication and self-restraint. Gluttony was seen as shameful: Louis XVI's eating habits, for example were recorded as 'scandalous'. The new eating body was a **civilized** body, shaped by the refinement of table manners and culinary skills. The concept of corporeal volume as a sign of prestige was supplanted by the fetish of the slim figure.

For the ancient Greeks and the early Christians, dieting was a way of achieving mastery over the flesh to help the soul or spirit develop. But from the nineteenth century onwards, dieting has aimed at remoulding the physical body itself. Today, slenderness is part and parcel of a massive dieting industry whose values mirror the values of our society as a whole.

Contemporary western and 'westernized' cultures are full of contradictions. They tell us we are free and self-determining, at the same time as they treat us as commodities. They ask us to consume lavishly as if there was no tomorrow, and yet to watch our bodies' every move. The body images which surround us are correspondingly **contradictory.** Take the ideal of the slim, boyish female body. This could be read as a casting off of the burden of traditional views of domestic and reproductive femininity. But it also reinforces the idea of woman as a fragile and defenceless being, a weaker vessel, especially in comparison with the resurgent muscularity of the ideal male body.

Eating disorders reflect our culture's schizophrenic attitudes. The ***anorexic*** *body mirrors a work ethics of extreme self-discipline. The* ***obese*** *body symbolizes total self-indulgence. The* ***bulimic*** *body combines unrestrained consumption with drastic 'cleaning-up' practices. While obesity rejects mainstream images based on thinness-as-beauty, anorexia pays them homage to monstrous extremes. The anorexic body strives to live up to the standards of perfection promoted by advertizing. But it also attacks the idea of woman as a reproductive being driven by bestial hunger. And, finally, it is a tragic way of* ***proving oneself*** *through manic control over one's body and its most basic requirements.*

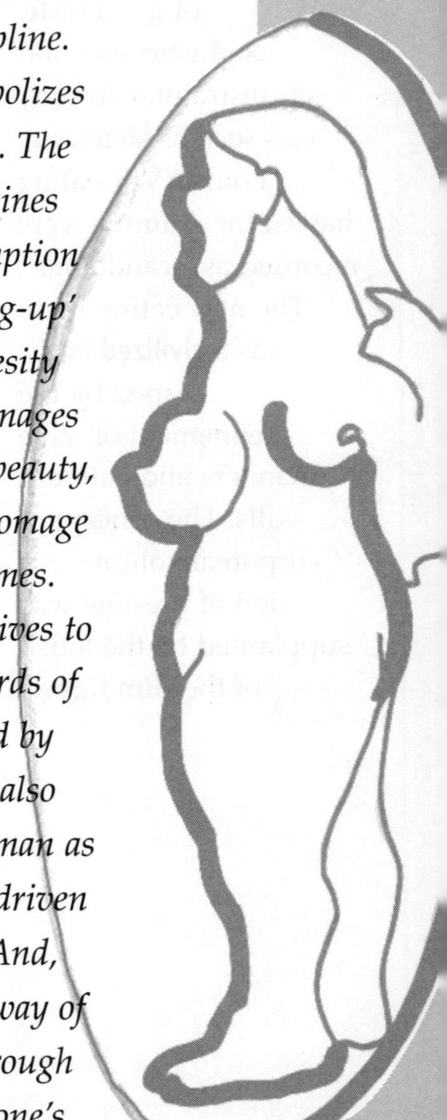

clothed bodies

Just as food isn't something we merely consume to keep our bodies alive, so clothes aren't things we wear just to keep our bodies warm or cool. Clothes help us make statements about our sexuality, age, social standing and political convictions. Through the selection and combination of particular items and styles, dress speaks a **language** which can be explored and taken apart just as verbal and written languages can. The language of dress has changed dramatically over time, in much the same way as the language of food has.

An extreme case was the wearing of deliberately uncomfortable garments to curb the body and its carnal desires. The Renaissance saw a momentous increase in bodily decoration. Physical bulk was amplified through the proliferation of layers of fabric which made dress undistinguishable from ***theatrical costume.*** *This was, after all, a culture of spectacle and display. Funnily enough, the padding out of the body through sumptuous clothing often had the effect not of magnifying the body but of making it appear frail and insubstantial under all that weight.*

The Middle Ages placed great emphasis on the soul and saw the body as its temporary dwelling place. Clothing was a means of displaying inner spiritual characteristics through material symbols.

In the eighteenth century, the development of internal markets and trade with the New World made a growing range of exciting products available. The attitude to fashion became ambivalent. On the one hand, people were obsessed with the idea of refinement as a marker of taste and condemned sartorial excess. On the other, clothing was seen as a way of expressing one's affluence and prestige.

Contemporary culture is no less schizophrenic. Mass-production has democratized fashion: the aristocracy is no longer the trend-setter. Yet, we are conditioned by other forces, such as the cult of the designer, and addicted to new role models, such as film and pop stars. We still use clothes to show how we perceive our bodies and how we wish to be perceived by others. Clothes **make us***. The verb 'to fashion', after all, means 'to shape', 'to mould'.*

But how does a body go about **choosing** its clothes? The fashion industry supplies ambiguous guidelines. It advertizes its products as seductive innovations, yet it keeps recycling familiar ideas with only minimal differences. Fashionable outfits, or costumes, help us toy with different body images and alternative identities. But there is nothing truly new about any of the images we adopt because we are driven all the time by one and the same imperative: **reinventing our bodies.**

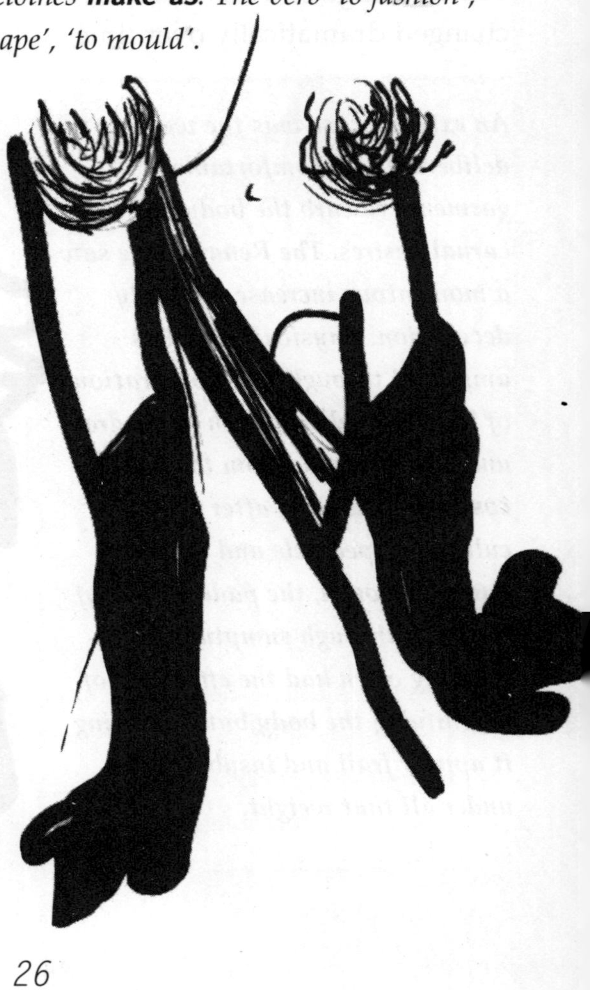

Fashion tells us that our bodies can stand out as special and unique at the same time as it fosters uniformity. We often wear certain garments because we want our bodies to be **different.**

But we also wish to belong to a community of style.

Dress also makes us aware of the instability of our bodily boundaries. Clothes ***frame*** *the body and separate it from others. But they simultaneously help one body relate to another body as a kind of* ***connecting tissue****. We relate to others whenever we recognize what they are wearing.*

Clothes are both a part and not a part of the physical body. On the one hand, they are detachable from the physical shape. But on the other, they complete the body in vital ways. We could hardly perform, especially in public, without some artificial casing. Some have actually described the body as a **peg** for clothing. Others have argued that the body is no more solid than a piece of fabric, that the body itself is a **garment.** Clothes lend substance to our flimsy bodies to the point that they become a substitute **skin**. The sensuous, tactile properties of different materials - softness, smoothness, toughness, prickliness, etc. - can contribute crucially to our sense of the erotic.

According to some anthropological theories, the origin of dress was magical. Clothes, particularly those made from animal hides, were a means of magnetizing positive animistic energies and warding off negative ones. We may no longer think of clothes as magical, yet many of us still talk of the 'lucky' dress to be worn as a talisman on challenging occasions. We are still superstitious about what we wear and about its influence on our bodies.

sex/porn/eros

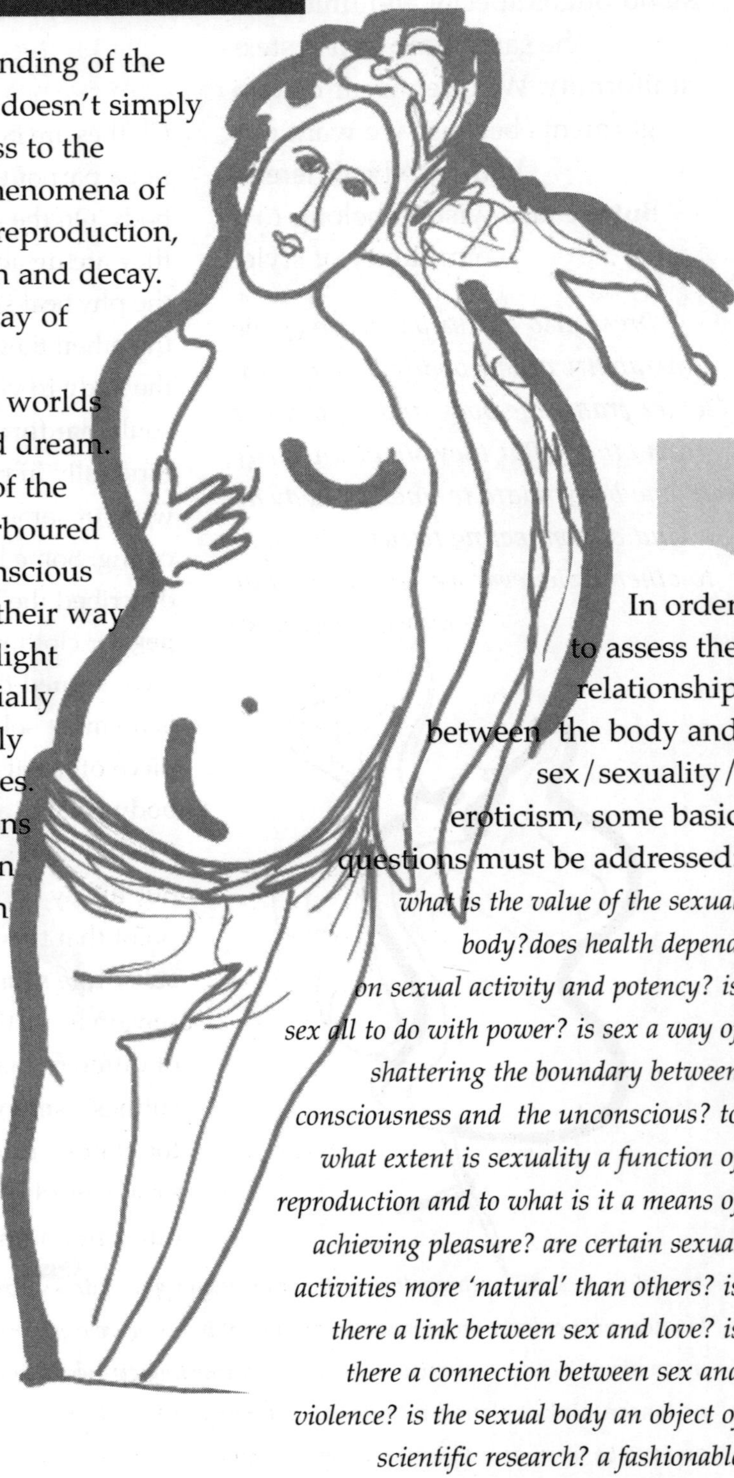

An understanding of the sexual body doesn't simply give us access to the biological phenomena of conception, reproduction, birth, growth and decay. It is also a way of probing the unconscious worlds of desire and dream. Only a few of the fantasies harboured by the unconscious mind make their way into the daylight realm of socially and culturally shared images. Large portions of the hidden mind remain untapped.

In order to assess the relationship between the body and sex/sexuality/eroticism, some basic questions must be addressed: *what is the value of the sexual body? does health depend on sexual activity and potency? is sex all to do with power? is sex a way of shattering the boundary between consciousness and the unconscious? to what extent is sexuality a function of reproduction and to what is it a means of achieving pleasure? are certain sexual activities more 'natural' than others? is there a link between sex and love? is there a connection between sex and violence? is the sexual body an object of scientific research? a fashionable commodity? is it a 'myth'?*

The word 'sex' comes from the Latin *secare*: 'to separate'. We are often told that sex enables people to experience a sense of total **fusion.** But the origin of the word suggests that bodies are actually 'separated' by sex. And indeed, conventional ways of organizing sexuality have relied heavily on oppositions: certain bodies penetrate, others get penetrated, for example. The concept of division also obtains on the biological level: certain bodies produce fattening hormones (e.g. estrogen) meant to aid child-bearing and nursing, others produce muscle-building hormones (e.g. testosterone) meant to fuel aggressivity and the desire for possession.

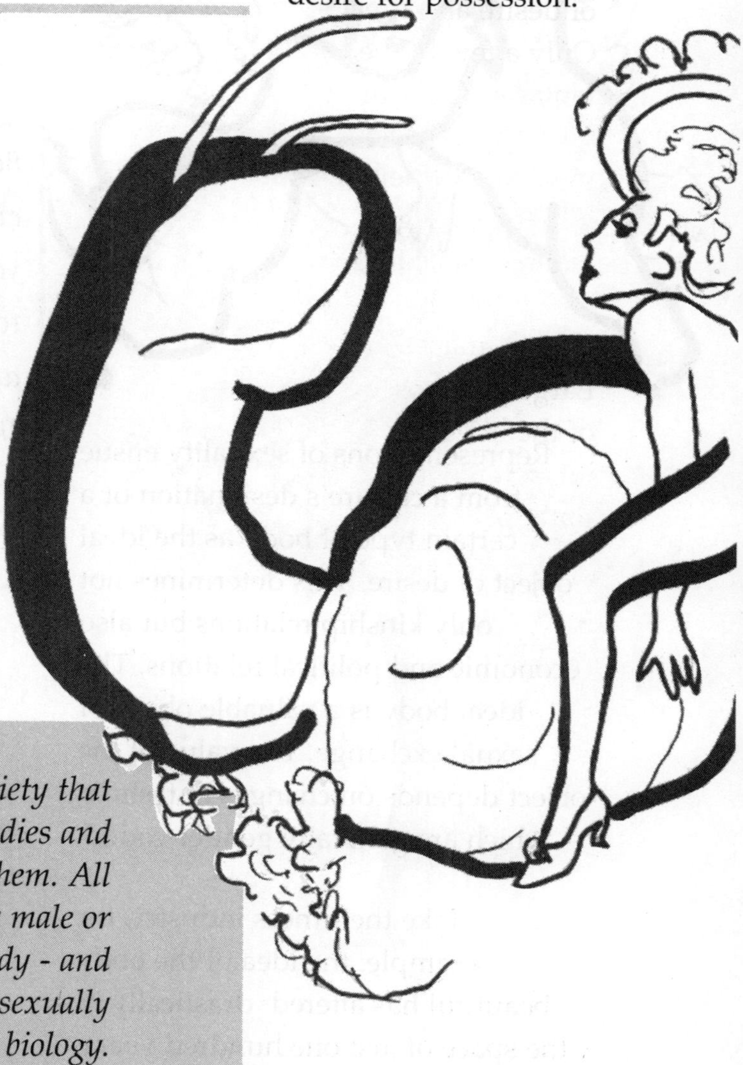

But ultimately it is society that makes both sexual bodies and distinctions amongst them. All bodies are biologically male or female but no body - and ***nobody*** *- is sexually predetermined by biology.*

Many cultural factors create the sexual body quite regardless of that body's biological gender: ideas about beauty, emotions, creativity, familial responsibilities, work and professional success, to mention but a few.

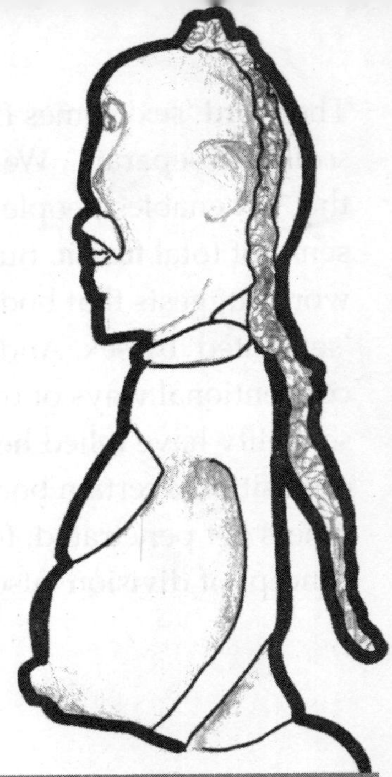

Body images are always cultural fabrications, yet we are encouraged to take them for granted as if they were natural. This process of naturalization gives rise to legion stereotypes.

Representations of sexuality ensue from a culture's designation of a certain type of body as the ideal object of desire. This determines not only kinship relations but also economic and political relations. The ideal body is a valuable object of sexual exchange. The value of the object depends on changes in fashion which are generally gender-coded.

Take the fitness industry, for example: the idea of the body beautiful has altered drastically in the space of just one hundred years.

In the nineteenth century, physical fitness was seen as a masculine endowment. It spelled out virility and boldness. A female bodybuilder would have been regarded as a freak. Today, fitness is associated with physical dexterity rather than sheer strength. 'Working out', combined with mental determination, could even be a means of **making** it in a competitive world: think of the film **Flashdance** as a case in point. The contemporary 'fit' body is a complex compound. It is a **celebrated** body. But it is also an **enduring** body produced through training and meant to compete beyond the pain threshold; a body in jeopardy, produced by putting the body at risk in the quest for excitement; a **muscular** body; a **sculpted** body.

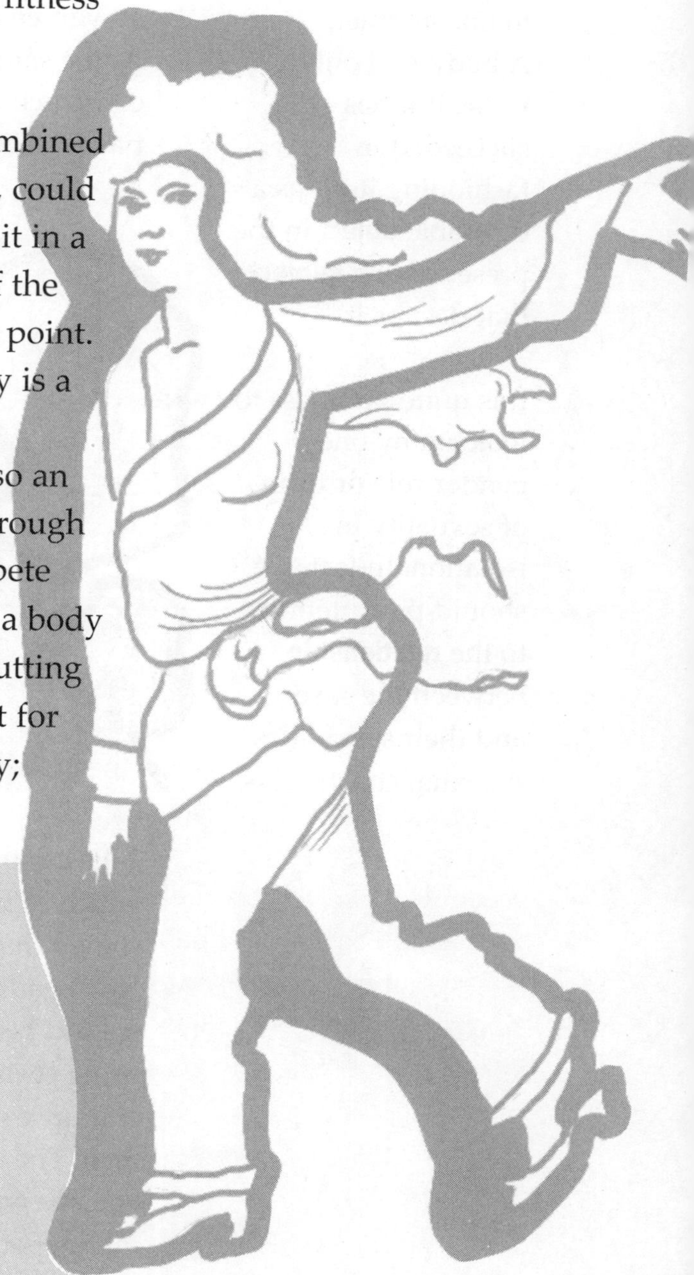

The sexual bodies constructed by a society never exist as separate objects. They only gain meaning in relation to one another. A body will only know if it has succeeded in fashioning itself as a desirable **object** in the presence of a **subject** that desires it.

It is quite pointless to look at any one gender role or form of sexuality in isolation. In fact, we should pay attention to the **relationship** between the sexes and their sexualities. A sexual construct is the spin-off of another construct. Think, for example, of the stereotype of the 'cool' male, expected to avoid seeming intentionally concerned with attracting women. This image of masculinity licenses certain men to stare at women in any available situation. At the same time, it fuels another construct: the image of woman as a passive object of the male gaze.

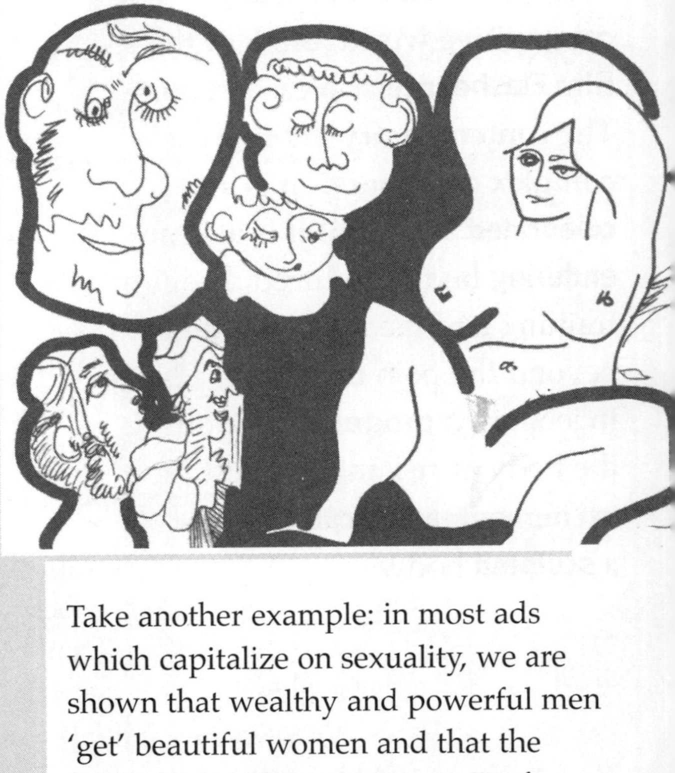

Take another example: in most ads which capitalize on sexuality, we are shown that wealthy and powerful men 'get' beautiful women and that the reward beautiful women receive for being sexually attractive is that they end up with wealthy and powerful men. The images of the sexy woman and the well-to-do man are interdependent. Similarly, in the Victorian period, a woman was supposed to be something of a **fashion plate**, designed to advertise her husband's prosperity. Beauty and status depended on each other to communicate certain cultural values. Neither would mean much separately from the other.

Sexual glamour is a function of status. Status, in turn, is governed by economic and financial imperatives but also relies on **visual** dominance. It is connected with the possession of commodities but also with the appropriation of the 'right' to look at other people as though they, too, were consumer products.

If the sexual body is a cultural construct, and if the ideal sexual body changes radically through time, who can tell what **natural** sexuality is? Can anybody establish if there is such a thing? Ongoing debates about pornography highlight these issues.

Conventionally, pornography is equated to obscenity: films, photographs and books which deal with bodily acts considered indecent by the public. But clearly attitudes change. Materials deemed obscene by the Victorians may not be considered even remotely offensive today. Works of literature once suppressed by anti-porn laws, such as James Joyce's **Ulysses** (1922), D.H. Lawrence's **Lady Chatterley's Lover** (1928), and Vladimir Nabokov's **Lolita** (1955), are now taught on canonical syllabuses. These fluctuations in the public perception of the obscene still make pornography extremely hard to define.

Pornography also seems to defy **legal** description. In 1957, the U.S. Supreme Court tried to set legal guidelines for defining obscenity. It came up with three rules: pornography appeals to prurient interests, it offends current standards of taste, and it has no redeeming social value. The difficulty with this definition is that it assumes a universal consensus amongst people about what is *prurient*, *offensive* or *redeeming*. As it happens, these concepts are very relative and by no means natural. The Williams Report, published in Britain in 1979, presents similar problems. It states that pornography is offensive to reasonable people, that public display of obscene materials is unacceptable but private consumption is legitimate, and that pornography arouses people through explicit sexual content. But the report doesn't tell us, regrettably, what is meant by *reasonable, public, private, arousing* or *explicit.* All these terms remain unexplained. There are no unchanging criteria for drawing the line between what's acceptable and what isn't.

Nor is it viable to talk of 'arousal' in the abstract. We must scrutinize the **techniques** through which it is accomplished. Sexual images don't produce sexual excitement simply by portraying unclothed bodies. The sexual organs would be of limited interest were it not for the **poses** adopted by the models and for the costumes and gadgets employed to back them up. The body must be **put on display**, as an object ready for consumption. Lasciviously reclining bodies, handcuffed and tied-up bodies, bodies on all fours and bodies thrusting out provocatively parts of their anatomy are not just 'naked'. They are naked for a **purpose**: exploiting our desire.

Some psychologists believe that the sexual abuse of women and children is a direct result of sadistic porn. Others argue that there is no obvious link between the consumption of porn and violent or antisocial behaviour. Others still think that some men develop negative attitudes towards women as a result of their exposure to violence, especially through films, even if the content of these films is not overtly sexual.

In recent years, many have tried to extend the debate on pornography into a broader examination of power structures. They have looked at the ways in which the exploitation of women as sexual objects relates to the violation of other marginal groups: feminine, black, poor or weak men, for instance. The denigration of the female body has been observed in conjunction with the abuse of all forms of ***otherness.*** *This suggests that we cannot address sexual relations as an issue separate from the rest of the culture in which they occur. Sexual relations reflect, and often* ***condense,*** *wider social relations.*

Some have tried to define pornography by contrast with **erotica**. They argue that erotica is based on a celebration of the body and reciprocity of pleasure, whereas pornography is based on the subjection of one party by another. If the work is simply intended to titillate, it can be dismissed as trash. If it explores human sexuality, it escapes condemnation. But these matters are vague. Not everybody views explicit representations of the sexual body as demeaning or exploitative. Many people actually believe that both erotica and porn are a means of exposing hypocritical moral standards: of pulling to the surface forbidden longings which lurk beneath a culture's veneer of 'propriety'.

Others think that images of the sexual body are healthy in that they compel us to confront our **irrational** side, and so challenge the smug notion of human beings as rational animals.

Moreover, many non-western cultures possess ancient traditions of explicitly erotic art which may or may not be considered obscene. Indian representations of sexuality are often based on the idea that orgasm is a form of spiritual enlightenment, a way of bridging the gap between the human and the divine. In Chinese tradition, the fusion of **yin** and **yang** (the feminine and the masculine) is a means of achieving not only pleasure but also physical and psychological health. Both traditions see the universe as inexhaustibly fertile.

We shouldn't forget that sexuality has been ingrained in the visual arts since the beginning of time. Stone Age artists were already carving female shapes with magnified sexual attributes, possibly to celebrate fertility, and possibly to stimulate erotic desire.

But the sexual dimension of various cultures has often been repressed. When most of us are taught about the ancient Egyptians, for instance, much is said about pyramids and about the divine bodies of Pharaohs and their wives. The sexual images so vital to the whole of Egyptian religion and cosmology are hardly ever mentioned. The orgies that accompanied planting and harvesting rituals are generally not mentioned **at all!**

In marginalizing the sexual body, history has laid an especially heavy ban on **female** bodies. Yet ancient civilizations are packed with powerful female deities presiding over the fertility not just of women but of whole countries. The Egyptian earth goddess **Isis** and the Babylonian love goddess **Ishtar**, for instance, dominated important cults, involving overtly sexual performance.

Greek culture was keen on principles of rationality and harmony. Its official religion associated female sexuality with a delicate and thoroughly 'feminine' Venus. But on the periphery of Olympus, women could still find an outlet for their wildest sexual emotions in the cult based on the god **Dionysus**. The god's followers, known as **Maenads** or **Bacchae**, took part in ecstatic rituals involving inebriation, dancing, suckling leopard and wolf cubs, tearing animals apart and consuming their raw flesh. This may sound a bit 'extreme'. But it also goes to show that cultures are never quite successful in taming irrational drives. They may produce sanitized versions of the sexual body. Yet they cannot ultimately enforce one type of sexuality to the exclusion of all others. Erotic urges cannot be legislated away.

But western culture still labours under the curse of the Fall **legend, where the villains of the piece are the woman** Eve **and a reptilian** Devil**. What could poor, 'innocent'** Adam **do in such dubious company?...**

The denial of the sexual body reached its peak in the Middle Ages. Eroticism was stunted and demonized. Yet many pictures of the period, in displaying gutted martyrs, bleeding and dismembered sinners burning in hell, and gory torture chambers, show a deep obsession with the body's physicality. The artists that painted those images may well have been thinking: if the body is capable of producing such a range of 'nasty' effects, isn't there a chance that it may be capable of producing as many **pleasurable** ones?

The fact remains that throughout western civilization, the bias against the sexual body has resulted from the cultural construction of female sexuality as a corrupting agency.

This image enjoyed great popularity in the nineteenth century. If one side of the Victorian mentality liked to think of woman as the 'angel in the house', as a helpless child, a nun-like virgin, or an invalid, the other side saw woman as predatory, voracious and driven by an insatiable hunger for seed. Guides to married life actually called the woman who expected to have sexual intercourse more than once a fortnight, a vampire, eager to drain her husband of all vitality

Female sexuality has been regarded as a destructive force largely because it has been subliminally associated with the animal phenomenon of **estrus,** or **'heat'**. In certain species, a female in heat is driven into such a state of hormonal frenzy as to be capable of having intercourse dozens of times in the course of one single day with several males. The human female is often equated to her bestial counterpart. Some cultures curb female sexuality through **clitorectomy** (or 'female circumcision'), which consists of the surgical removal of the clitoris, and **infibulation**, in which the outer lips of the female organ are stitched together.

But mutilation is not always physical. It can also be psychological: women may be brainwashed into believing that maternal and domestic duties, not the pursuit of bodily pleasures, are their 'true' vocation.

The sexual body can be physically manipulated. But it can also, no less importantly, be disciplined through language. Often, it is not the material body itself that is repressed but the words and phrases that refer to bodily functions. The physical things we feel most embarrassed about are displaced onto the plane of linguistic embarrassment.

Take the language of obscenity...

taboos

The most common swear words refer to basic bodily functions: sex and excretion. In our culture, these functions are taboo and the language that relates to them also becomes taboo.

All taboos are connected with the body. Tabooed behaviour and language most often apply to things that are borderline, that cannot be straightforwardly classified. The corpse is tabooed because of its nebulousness. It is both a body and not a body, a person and not a person. It is an object that we cannot name for it lacks the body's essence - life - yet it still retains the external appearance of a body.

The gap between life and death, this world and the other world is filled with taboos. Religions have tried to bridge it by inventing bodies that are both human and non-human, such as incarnate gods, virgin mothers and hybrid monsters.

Bodily secretions and exudations are the object of severe censorship because they are ambiguous. They remind us that our physical boundaries are precarious.

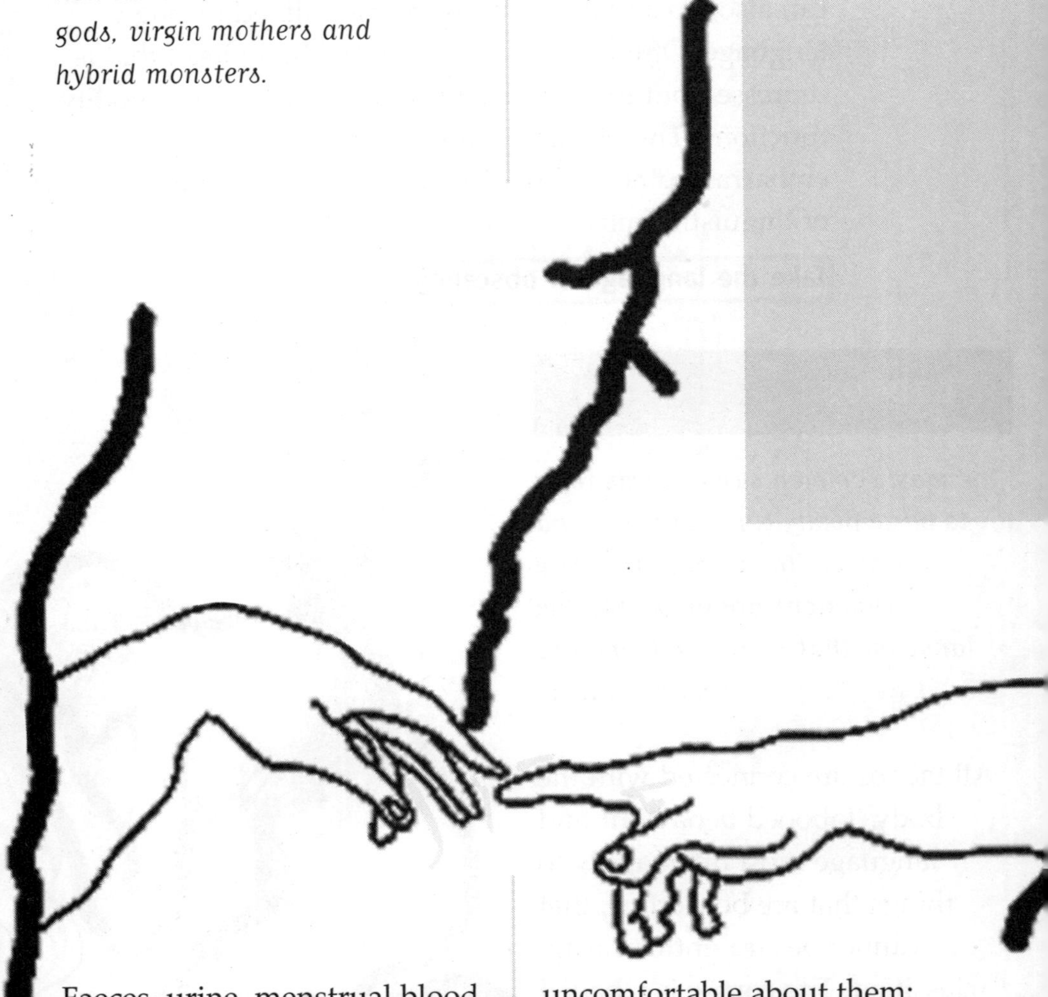

Faeces, urine, menstrual blood, semen, nail parings, spittle, sweat, dead hair, tears, flakes of dry skin, maternal milk, sebum are both inside and outside the body. We are unable to allocate these substances to one definite place and this makes us uncomfortable about them: as a result, we consign them to the shadowy territory of taboo. Interestingly, however, many of these substances were once regarded as the principal ingredients of magical medicine.

A form of obscene language as widespread as that surrounding basic bodily functions is that of animal abuse. Western thought has always been keen on asserting the superiority of human beings to other animals. Making certain animals **obscene** *is a way of strengthening that belief. Funnily enough, not all animals fit the bill. To call someone a 'son of a giraffe' rather than a 'son of a bitch' would hardly have the same effect - any more than substituting 'you antelope' for 'you swine' would. Maybe 'bitch' and 'swine' are more effective because they are explicitly associated with tabooed bodily activities: with filth and excretement, females on heat, mindless flesh grovelling in its own waste. The most overtly physical and animalistic aspects of the body meet the harshest linguistic censorship.*

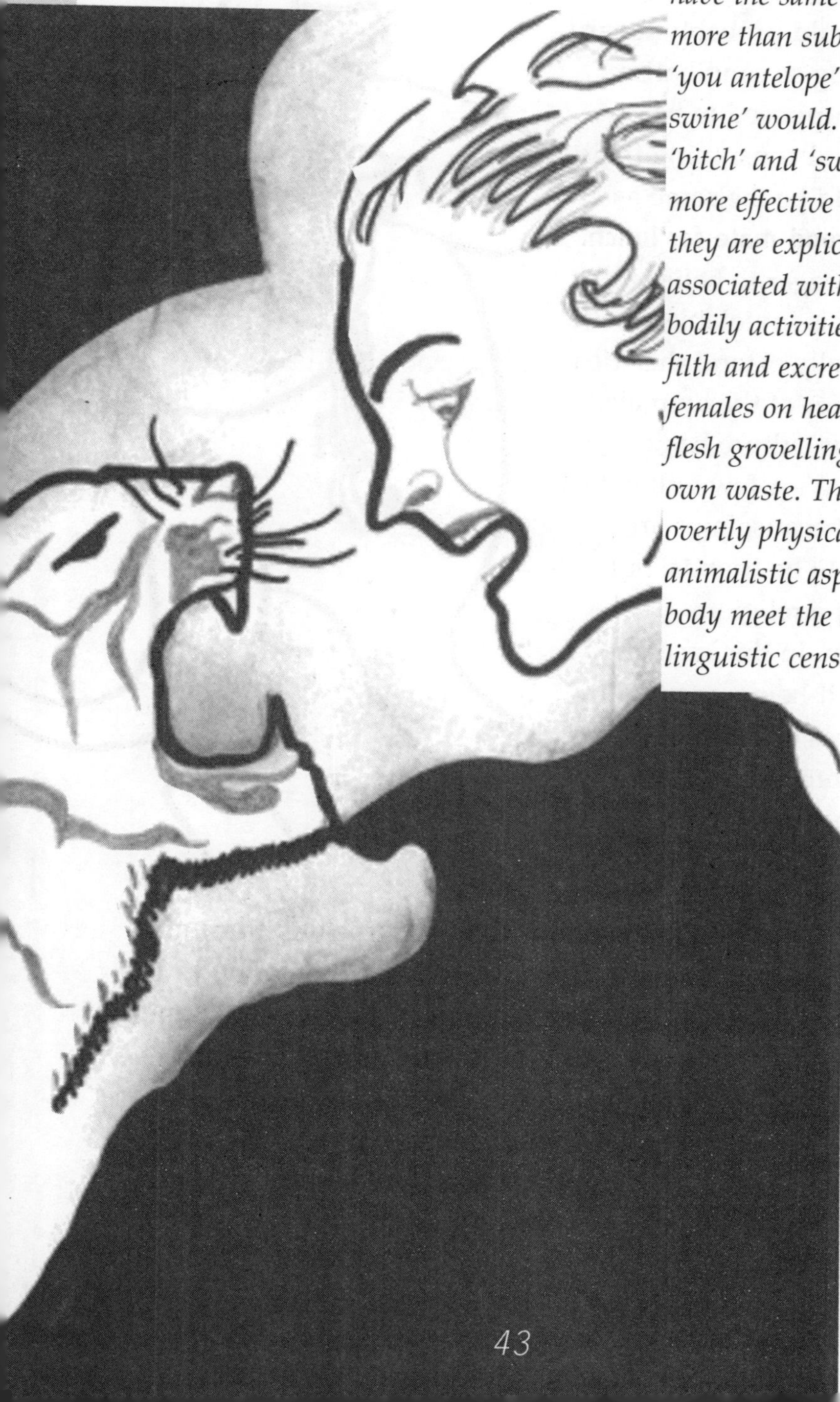

Many of the ways in which we talk about animals and use them - as pets, labour or food - reflect our ways of thinking about our own bodies and their taboos. These vary hugely from culture to culture. An English person would probably regard eating a dog as cannibalism: dogs are supposed to be 'friends' and consuming their meat would be the same as **having a good mate for lunch**. If you are eager to believe that your body is inviolable, you'll automatically extend this idea to the bodies of the animals which your culture has 'humanized'. A Jew will not eat pork: not because pigs are supposed to be friends, but because of a religious prohibition. In this case, the body's well-being, secured by what it does or does not ingest, is a guarantee of spiritual wholesomeness.

Whenever we define ourselves through animals, we also repress animality. In the English person's case, the pet is stripped of its animality by being turned into an honorary human. In the Jew's case, the animal's forbidden meat is not just matter but a spiritual idea. Either way, animality becomes taboo.

There are parallels between eating habits and sexual codes and conventions. We decide whether or not certain animals can be eaten in much the same way as we decide what sorts of people we can have sexual intercourse with. We assume that pets are inedible because they are close to us; that tame farm animals are unproblematically edible because they are bred to be eaten, although they are quite close to us; that game animals can be eaten but, since they are not tame, their availability as food cannot be taken for granted; and that totally wild animals are beyond our control and therefore inedible.

Similar rules guide our sexual conduct. We don't 'normally' have sex with our brothers and sisters any more than we treat our pets as food: they are too close to us. In some cultural groups, marriages between cousins are perfectly acceptable: they are meant to maintain certain familial structures and traditions. Cousins are the equivalent of farm animals: they are quite close but may intermarry if they have been raised for that purpose. We assume that we can have sexual intercourse with people who are not kin in any way: as with game animals, we cannot predict our chances. There is no taboo at work, but there is no guarantee of success either. Finally, we couldn't even begin to consider sex with totally unknown, distant strangers any more than we would think of eating zebras in the zoos.

Western culture encourages us to repress our commonality with other animals, largely by tabooing the life of the senses. But there is a trend, known as **animalism**, *which argues that humans are simply animals.*

Our identities can only be described in physical terms. Psychological criteria are something of a waste of time. Any sense of continuity in our lives has to do with the endurance of the animal body. When our bodies stop, so do we. Survival has nothing to do with mental functions such as memory.

Some philosophers have questioned the animalist position. They don't believe that as long as the body is in one piece, a person's self automatically stays the same. They quote cases of split-brain patients, brain zaps and multiple-personality disorders, to show that even when there is bodily continuity, there is not necessarily a continuity of self, or of identity. In those cases, the body remains the same but the person doesn't. Two or more selves inhabit a single body.

The animalist position is helpful in emphasizing the importance of the physical body. The anti-animalist position is equally useful in reminding us that our identities, mental or corporeal, are never singular. If it is the case that we are animals, it is also the case that each of us is often several animals at once.

What we cannot dodge is the fact that both our ways of thinking about the body and our bodies themselves alter constantly. No discipline that concerns itself with the body offers a unified account of all its functions. There is no universal agreement, for example, over the relationship between the body and **medicine.**

the medical body

Nowadays, the term medicine often evokes a discipline based in high-tech institutions. The body is its passive object. Treatment involves probing the body to its innermost depths, categorizing it, objectifying it, confining it. Medicine is supposed to carry a body of scientific knowledge that can only be acquired through strictly specialized procedures.

Yet in most societies, even technologically advanced ones, there are forms of ***folk medicine,*** *healing practices that do not entail formal training and are passed on from person to* ***person****. Folk medicine, at its best, adapts to the needs and features of individual bodies.* ***Aromatherapy*** *follows similar lines: essential oils have unique characteristics but these can only affect individual bodies according to specific psychological and physiological profiles.*

In certain cultures, a key role is played by traditional medicine. **This form of medicine involves methods of training and some textual guideposts but does not use advanced technology as its main tool. The oldest forms of traditional medicine are magical and religious in nature. One of them is** shamanism, **a widespread phenomenon that can be found amongst Eskimos, Native American tribes of North and South America, Indonesians, Australian Aborigines, Indians, Koreans, and many African cultures.**

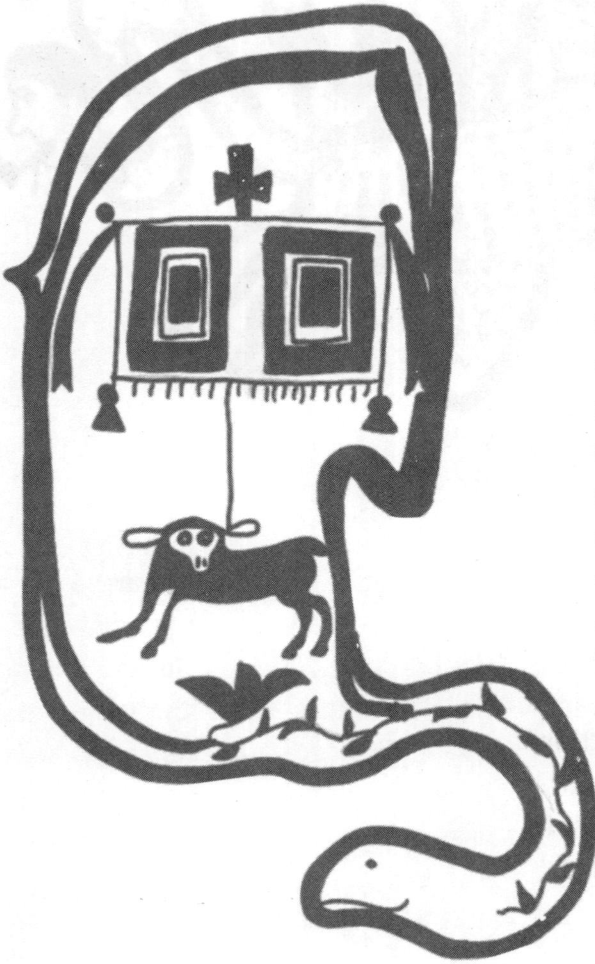

The shaman is endowed with the power to roam the spirit world and return to earth to cure the sick. Native Americans call shamans 'medicine men'; shamanistic figures in Africa are known as 'witch doctors'. Sickness is seen as a spiritual problem. When a soul is kidnapped by netherworld spirits, it is the shaman's task to restore it to its rightful body.

Other forms of traditional medicine view the body as a microcosm of the universe. In Indian **Ayurvedic** medicine, for example, the seven body substances (bone, flesh, fat, blood, semen, marrow and chyle) are the product of the three 'humours' (phlegm, bile and wind) which shape the world in its entirety. Health is the balance of these humours.

Galenic medicine, derived from the works of the ancient Greek doctor Galen, works along similar principles. There are four bodily humours (yellow bile, black bile, phlegm and blood) and these interact with environmental factors (heat, cold, moisture and dryness) to produce a healthy or an unhealthy body, depending on the balance of all the elements.

The concept of balance is also important in traditional Chinese medicine. The universe is controlled by yin **and** yang. **Yin is cold and female and represents the earth. Yang is hot and male and represents the heavens. A healthy body is one in which the levels of yin and yang are controlled and brought into equilibrium.**

Conventional medicine is by and large based on the idea of contrary medication. Illness is treated by administering the opposite substance to the one that is supposed to have caused it. Homeopathy, discovered by the German doctor Samuel Hahnemann in 1786, turned conventional medicine upside down by asserting that like cures like. Diseases are treated through substances similar to the ones that have brought them about in the first place.

Conventional medicine sees the sick body as a helpless thing. The body must be attacked by alien forces to be made well again. Homeopathy, by contrast, trusts the body's **self-healing** powers. Its substances increase slightly the symptoms of the illness, bring them out more clearly and so help the body recognize what's wrong and spring into action.

There is nothing mystical about this. Everyone knows that if the immune and defence systems are in good shape, the body will heal itself without recourse to science. If we are in reasonably good health, we don't need to see a professional over a mosquito bite. What homeopathy suggests is that we should give the body more credit for what it is able to do and allow it to take responsibility for its malfunctioning rather than treat it as a hopeless piece of meat.

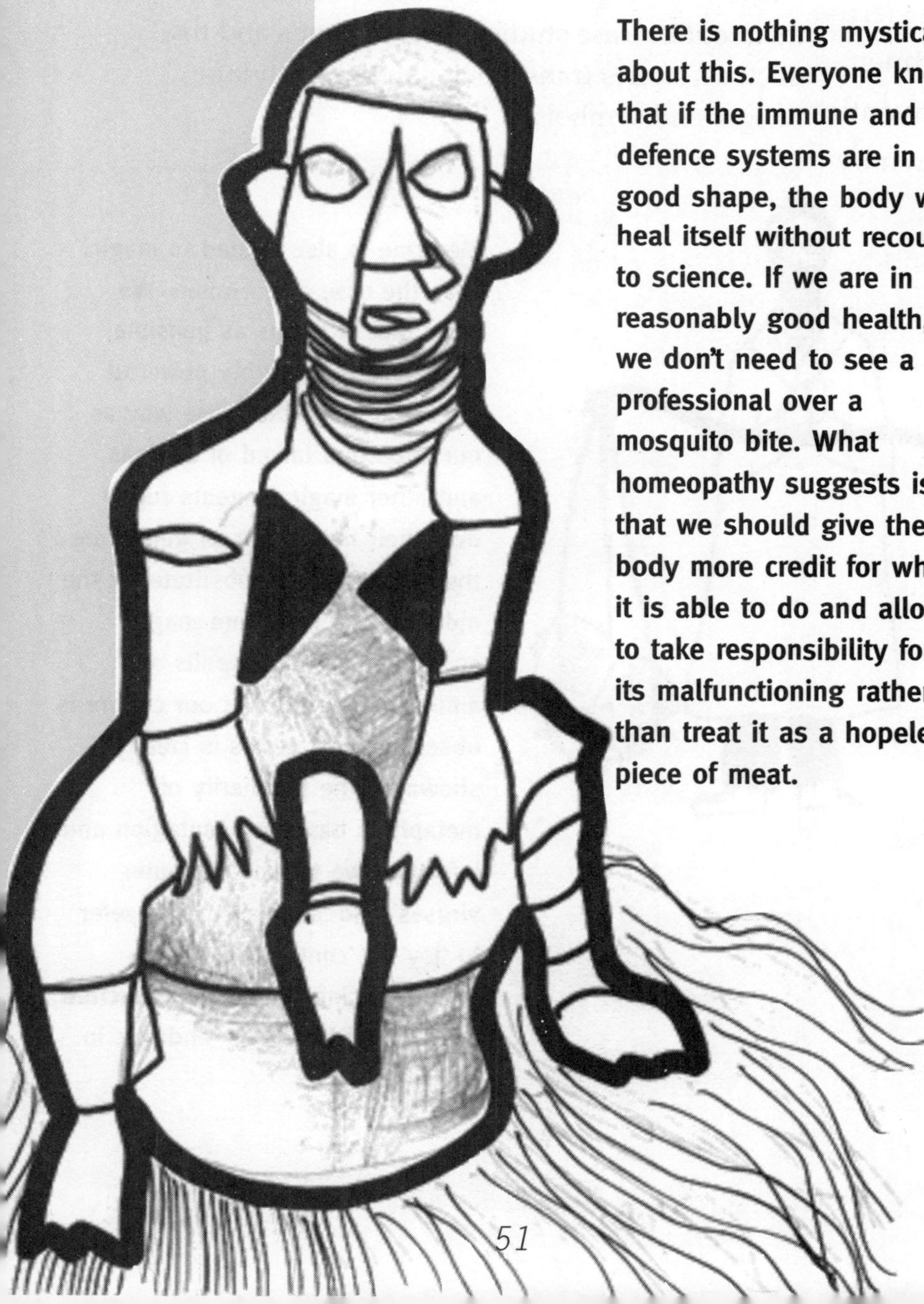

Science in general, and medicine in particular, are embroiled with the more ancient traditions of myth, legend and narrative. The medical experience is, after all, largely a matter of **story-telling.** Patients narrate their experiences to doctors. Narrative is a way of giving shape to their suffering. Doctors, too, tell stories when they diagnose their patients' illnesses and write them out as 'case studies'. The patient's and the doctor's stories translate the body's flesh into images and symbols.

Medicine is also related to magic. Take the case of germism**. We often talk of germs as invisible, capricious and terribly powerful forces, in much the same way as our ancestors talked of demons and other magical agents ruling over their lives. Just as germs are the contemporary substitute for the old spirits of myth and magic, so vaccines replace spells and amulets. The fact that our culture is obsessed with germs is clearly shown by the popularity of metaphors based on contagion and infection: we talk of 'computer viruses' and 'software bugs', refer to 'joy' as 'contagious' and to 'laugh' as 'infectious', and describe widespread trends as 'endemic in our society'.**

Germism proposes two versions of the body. There is the ***single*** body, based on an individualistic and proprietorial attitude towards illness: consider expressions such as 'my germ' or 'my bug'. And there is the ***collective*** body produced by the spreading of contaminative disease. The first type of body is insulated, the second porous. But germism also reflects a fundamentally ***xenophobic*** worldview.

The fear of physical contagion is also a metaphor for the fear of invasion, contamination and pollution of one culture by another. This explains why the images we use to describe illness are often based on the military notions of warfare, attack and counter-attack.

Medicine's complicity with mythical ideas is blatantly shown by conventional ways of thinking about disability. The bias against disabled people throughout history is clustered around the myth of the *body perfect.* **This case indicates that myths are not just ancient tales about heroes and supernatural beings. They are also the unexamined assumptions and opinions on which cultures found their belief systems.**

Traditionally, disability has been of scarce interest for sociologists, who have preferred to see it as a medical and psychological problem rather than a social issue. This attitude is a by-product of the lamentable tendency to take as the standard object of study the 'rational', 'whole' individual. Anything departing from that 'norm' is seen as either irrelevant or an instance of **outlandish** *behaviour. Disabled people's own productivity is generally ignored. As a result, common responses to disability have degenerated into mythical stereotypes: fear, revulsion, hostility, distrust, uneasiness, pity, and patronizing behaviour.*

But how is disability defined? Medically, it is negatively defined in terms of a biological or physiological inferiority, encapsulated by derogatory terms such as invalid, cripple, spastic, etc. The medical definition spills over into non-professional attitudes. These are predicated on discrimination, disempowerment, oppression and abuse. The public just doesn't know enough about disability and opts for the head-under-the-sand approach. It is easier to conceive of disabled people as threats to 'healthy' power relations or, at best, as pathetic freaks, than to address the issue of their place in society. Accepting that they *have* a place at all means also having to question the place of so-called *able* people, and hence rethinking the entire cultural paradigm.

If disability is perceived by many as a 'problem', this is not because disabled people are unable to adjust to the demands of society but because society repeatedly fails to adjust to the needs and aspirations of citizens with disabilities. More is needed than simply a widening of resources and access. It is not enough to supply the disabled with medical assistance. What is needed is a social structure in which people with disabilities may contribute more effectively to the medical and legal decisions which affect their status in society.

We should also stop using the term disability as a blanket category. Not all disabled people experience their impairments in the same ways. The disability movement has been gaining increasing strength as a social movement in contemporary culture, but it is important to appreciate differences within the movement itself. The implications of disability vary according to social and ethnic background, gender and sexual orientation. A serious study of the causes of marginalization within society requires an analysis of the different forms which victimization and isolation take in relation to other cultural factors. How a society excludes particular bodies on the basis of their disabilities speaks volumes about that society's understanding of what is acceptable and what isn't.

Disability is as old as humankind: archaeological evidence goes as far back as the Neanderthal period. But societal responses to people with impairments vary. In the late nineteenth century, a popular approach was the **surplus population theory**, which stated that when economic survival is precarious, weak bodies must be disposed of. Some cultures have seen impairment as a form of divine punishment or the outcome of witchcraft. Others have viewed the disabled as a gifted individual 'chosen' by God.

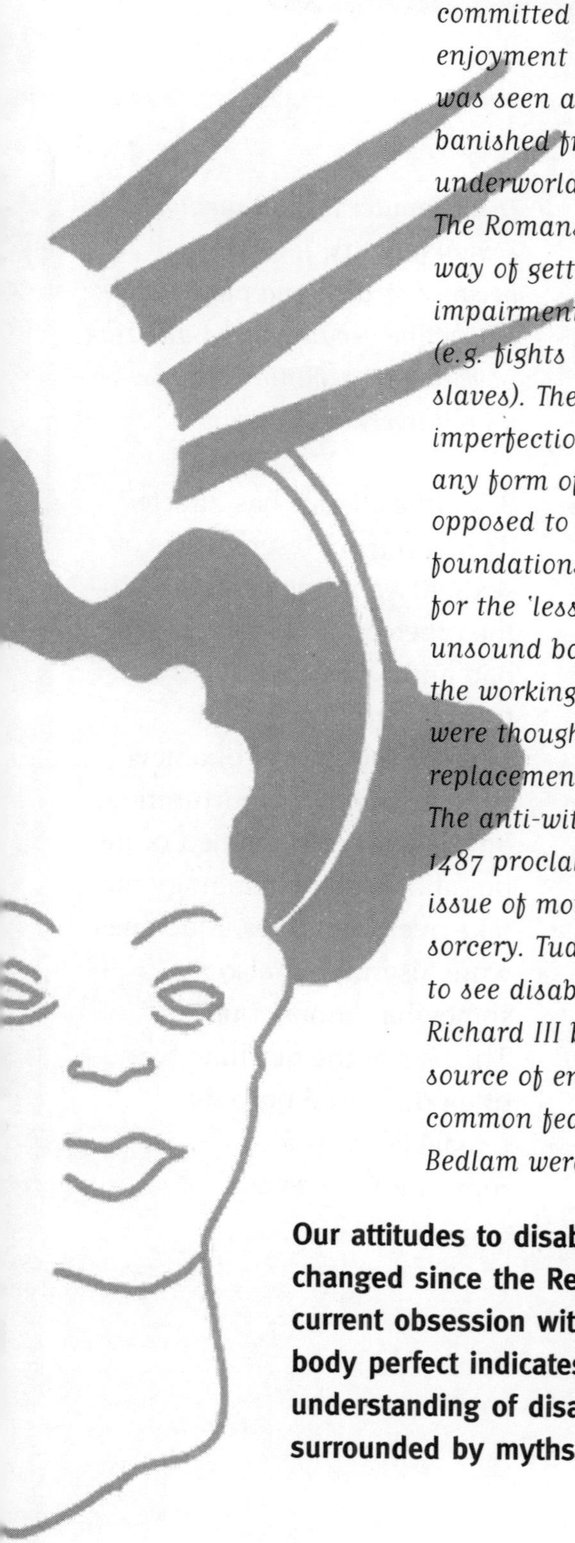

The Greeks were obsessed with fitness as necessary to the survival of a culture committed both to endless warfare and to the enjoyment of the physical world. Disability was seen as ungodlike: Hephaestes was banished from Olympus and confined to the underworld because of his lameness.

The Romans were keen on infanticide as a way of getting rid of sickly bodies, and turned impairment into a form of spectacle (e.g. fights between dwarfs and female slaves). The Jewish **Leviticus** catalogued imperfections which excluded people from any form of religious ritual. Yet Judaism was opposed to infanticide and laid the foundations for the Christian cult of caring for the 'less fortunate'. In the Middle Ages, unsound bodies were taken as evidence for the workings of Satan: visibly frail children were thought of as changelings, the Devil's replacements for human children.

The anti-witchcraft **Malleus Maleficarum** of 1487 proclaimed that such children were the issue of mothers who had dabbled with sorcery. Tudor and Stuart England continued to see disability as a sign of evil (King Richard III being a good example) and a source of entertainment: 'fools' were a common feature at Court and outings to Bedlam were popular.

Our attitudes to disability have obviously changed since the Renaissance. But the current obsession with the ideal of the body perfect indicates that the scientific understanding of disability is still surrounded by myths.

reproduction & the technobody

Technology has had a strong impact on our ways of thinking about the body in general and its reproductive function in particular. The biological organism is often compared to mechanical structures. For example, anatomy textbooks often liken the female body to a reproductive machine. Menstruation is described as failed production **or a** disused factory, **and menopause as a breakdown of** central control.

If the body can be talked about in technological terms, it is also the case that mechanical objects have often been invested with bodily and sexual attributes. The machines of the early industrial period are frequently associated with stereotypical ideas of masculinity and virility because of their thrusting energy, noisiness and impressive bulk. Electronic technology, on the other hand, is linked to feminine stereotypes because it is quiet, inconspicuous and miniaturized.

The computer has an ambiguous sexual identity: it is asexual because of its bland appearance, masculine because of its amazing powers, and feminine because of its relatively small size.

Scientific change has affected deeply our representations of sexuality and reproduction. In the nineteenth century, people had ambivalent attitudes towards machines: they relished the advent of a new age and of new opportunities but were also frightened of the possibility that technology may take over their lives. Machines were 'useful' but also somewhat 'monstrous'. The fear of the machine was often displaced onto the female body as a reproductive system.

Like the machine, woman was both alluring and threatening. She was seen as the generator of life but also as an uncanny being unable to generate any meaning in her own right. This spawned many negative images of the female body as overwhelming and unreliable. Science endeavoured to restrain it by tightly controlling its reproductive capacities. The stereotype of the **hysteric** was a product of these disciplinary practices.

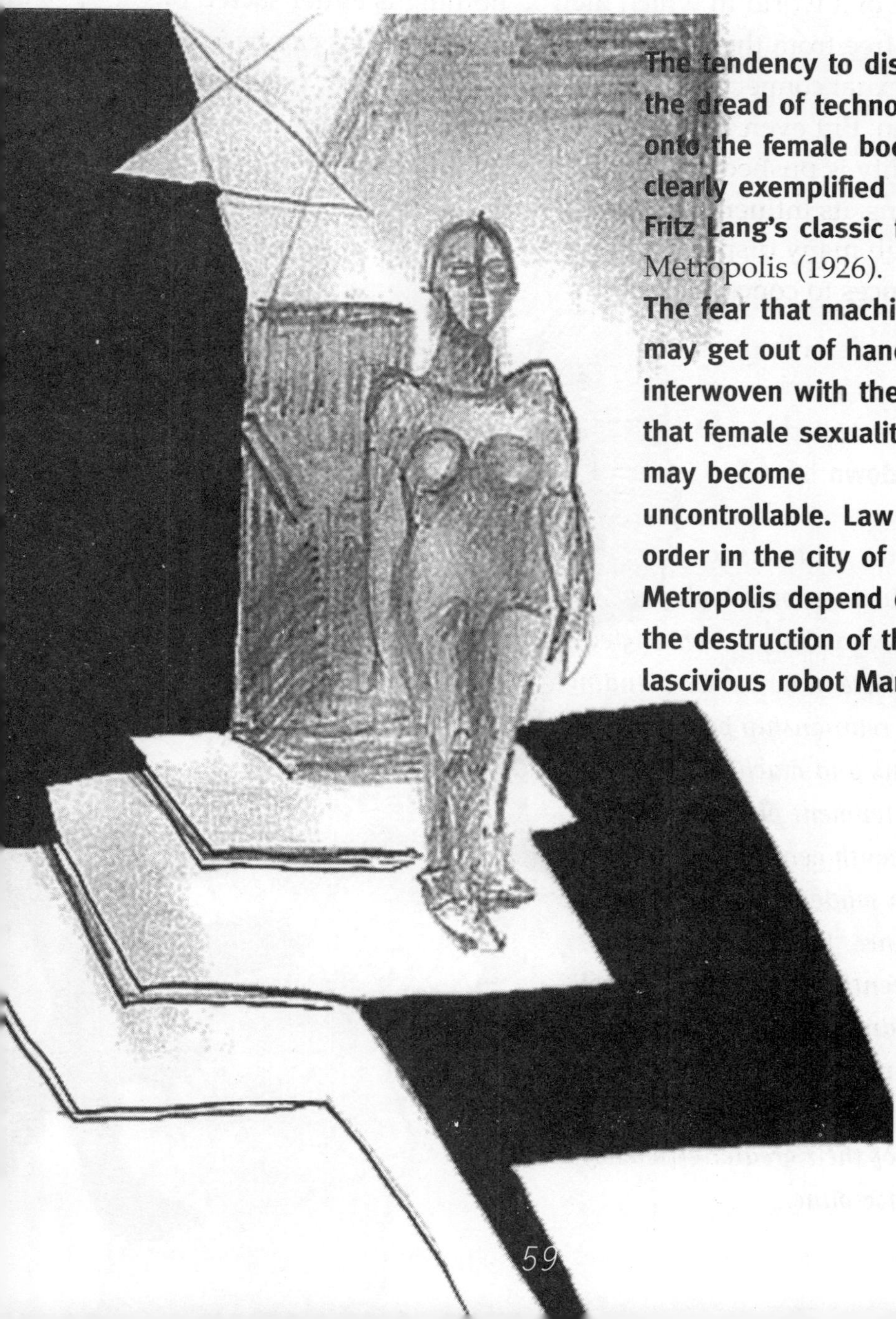

The tendency to displace the dread of technology onto the female body is clearly exemplified by Fritz Lang's classic film Metropolis (1926). **The fear that machines may get out of hand is interwoven with the fear that female sexuality may become uncontrollable. Law and order in the city of Metropolis depend on the destruction of the lascivious robot Maria.**

Conventionally, women are associated with biological reproduction and men with **technological** reproduction. Many sci-fi plots pivot on the idea that technology may wholly supplant the female reproductive function. They dream of a world in which men break free from their biological and sexual connections with women. But even as female sexuality is pushed to the margins, its influence persists through many displaced references to conception and procreation, in the disturbing forms of aliens and mutants. Horror films such as **Leviathan, The Fly, Alien, The Invasion of the Body Snatchers** articulate the fear of reproduction in relation to the theme of bodily invasion. They stress that nothing is either sacred or intact. Bodies can be invaded, contaminated, polluted. And birth is automatically related to the breeding of monsters.

Changing attitudes to reproduction, both biological and mechanical, are entangled with shifts in our understanding of the relationship between humans and machines. Enlightenment philosophy (eighteenth century) believed that reason made humans superior to machines. But in the late nineteenth century, the peak of the Industrial Revolution, machines were declared superior to the human body on the basis of their greater efficiency and discipline.

*Today, we seldom talk in terms of superiority and inferiority. We are more concerned with the **fusion** of the biological and the mechanical. It is becoming increasingly hard to separate 'real' bodily acts from artificially simulated ones.*

*A fairly extreme example of the body's penetration by technology is virtual sex: the sexual games in which we can participate through computers. This form of sexuality makes the physical body quite peripheral, if not downright redundant. In the film **Lawnmower Man**, for example, virtual sex is much more powerful than physical sex. Pleasure lies with the thrill of technology rather than a bodily act. Regular users of the CD-ROM programme **Virtual Valerie** say that they derive far more excitement from entering Valerie's apartment, roaming around the rooms and playing with various gadgets than they do from penetrating her with a dildo activated by moving the mouse backwards and forwards.*

*As pleasure becomes an effect of invisible electronic powers, the body is less and less central to sexuality. But this doesn't mean that sexual fantasies disappear. Rather, they are transformed and this transformation reflects a whole new order of experiences, cultural expectations and concepts of embodiment - in a word, **the technobody.***

the Body and philosophy

Outline

In philosophy, the relationship between mind and body has often been a controversial issue. Traditionally, the body has been associated with animal instincts and subordinated to intellectual and spiritual activities.
But increasingly, throughout the twentieth century, philosophers have argued that the body is central to our experience and knowledge of the world - that we only function insofar as we are **embodied** beings.

the mind-body problem

The relationship between the body and the mind is one of philosophy's most intractable concerns. The German philosopher **Arthur Schopenhauer (1788-1860)** called the mind-body problem 'the world knot': a puzzle beyond human comprehension.

How are physical processes related to mental processes?

How are sensory experiences translated into mental experiences, and vice versa?

For instance, in a hot environment, we may long for a drink of water: heat stimulates our senses in such a way that we experience the physical sensation of thirst. What is it, however, that makes us mentally conscious of the feeling of thirst, and guides us to water? How does a bodily desire like thirst manage to trigger the 'right' sets of neurons in the brain?

Mainstream western thought has generally seen the body as inferior to the mind. This trend can be traced at least as far back as **Plato (5th century B.C.).** The Greek philosopher played a key role in establishing the idea that material forms are flawed. The only truth, he argued, lives in the world of **Pure Forms**, that is disembodied ideas. Bodies are only second-rate 'copies' of that superior reality. Plato was also very anxious about heterosexual desire, which he saw as the cause of selfishness and envy. He was a lot more relaxed, however, on the subject of homosexual intercourse amongst men. He saw this as an encounter of 'beautiful souls', uncontaminated by the presence of woman.

Christianity has played no less significant a part in representing the body as imperfect, transitory and impure: **something to be ashamed of and transcended.**

One of the most influential figures in the mind-body debate was the French philosopher **René Descartes (1596-1650).** His system was based on the principle of 'dualism': body and mind are separate domains. The body is a material substance with physical properties such as shape, size and bulk; the mind is an immaterial substance with abstract properties such as thinking, feeling and willing. The mind is seen as superior to the body: pure knowledge, for Descartes, is achieved by disregarding the senses.

Descartes's most famous statement was: 'I think, therefore I am.' By this he meant that we exist because we are able to think. Our physical existence as bodies is quite irrelevant. Descartes also argued that the self is an 'object' that persists through time and that we pick out this object whenever we use the word 'I'. Yet he didn't explain what kind of an object the self is supposed to be. Of course deciding what counts as an object is always tricky. We find it quite normal to call a brick an object. **But can we call a shadow or a hologram an object? Can the self be an object without a body?**

One of the most radical assaults on Descartes's ideas came from **Friedrich Nietzsche (1844-1900)**. He maintained that rationalism asserted itself at the expense of the body. According to Nietzsche, abstract concepts such as thought and reason are actually functions of biology. We think the way we do because of the kinds of bodies we have. Knowledge springs from corporeal needs and interests. If we had a different kind of biology, the rest of the world would be different, too.

Yet civilization has insistently repressed the body's powers. Moral, religious and scientific laws have endeavoured to make the body weak and impotent by teaching us to be humble, obedient and servile. In repressing the body, civilization has made us ashamed of our instincts and denied our creativity.

The main target of Nietzsche's philosophy was the army of thinkers, artists and writers who despised, tamed, castrated and desensualized the body. For the German philosopher, these violations of the body have resulted from the 'will-to-truth': the desire to turn the randomness of human existence into a fixed meaning. Hatred for the body is a product of the desire to make everything practical, comprehensible and exploitable.

Nietzsche was especially dissatisfied with the hypocrisy and puritanism of the German middle class and its views on art and education. This class looked at Classical Greece as a model of virtue, order and self-restraint. But Nietzsche didn't believe that the artistic experience was all a matter of rational speculation and peace. In fact, he thought that our responses to art have much in common with sexual rapture and with the body's sensual and erotic drives. He argued this point by showing that ancient Greek culture wasn't all about tranquillity and stability, but actually encompassed two conflicting forces:

the **Apollonian** and the **Dionysian**. The 'Apollonian' (from the god Apollo) denotes order, self-control, harmony, balance, and the mind.
The 'Dionysian' (from the god Dionysus) is related to irrationality, ecstasy, inebriation, the loss of individual identity, and the **body**. Both forces are at work in the production and consumption of art.
The Dionysian has been inhibited by a false sense of morality. The only way of redressing the balance is to laugh loud at rationalism's efforts and push the neglected body into the foreground of philosophical thought.

According to the German philosophers **Theodor Adorno (1903-69)** and **Max Horkheimer (1895-1973)**, rationalism of the kind preached by Descartes has cut human history in half, by celebrating the mind and repressing the life of the instincts, the senses, and bodily drives. Ultimately, this strategy is bound to boomerang against itself: the more we fool ourselves into believing that, as rational human beings, we can control nature, the more alienated we become. We cannot have any control over anything, not even our own bodies, as long as we exercise only half of our being, the rational part. Repressing our physical nature transforms us into commodities.

Many people would argue that a crucial turning point in our understanding of the body-mind relationship was the advent of psychoanalysis. The theories of Sigmund Freud (1856-1939) **were complex and controversial, but it cannot be denied that they altered many traditional ways of perceiving the body. For one thing, they made it practically impossible to think independently of sexuality by emphasizing that we are sexual bodies right from childhood. Adult sexuality is informed by acts discovered and performed in infancy, such as thumb-sucking. These acts provide the backdrop for subsequent variations.**

In Freudian psychoanalysis, the adult body always carries the traces of the child's body. Some of these traces are alive in our conscious minds. But large portions of the child's body inhabit the **unconscious.** The parts of our minds that cannot be carried into consciousness are related to instincts which adult society is not prepared to tolerate. Sexual drives, in particular, are the object of intense taboo.

The unconscious pursues the ***pleasure principle****: primitive instincts which seek gratification regardless of social consequences. The conscious, adult mind follows the* ***reality principle.***

This imposes constraints on the pleasure principle: it tells us that gratification must be delayed until the object of our desire can be realistically achieved according to socially acceptable norms.

The adult body comes to express its impulses as a result of its **psychosexual** development throughout childhood. Developing bodies go through three phases. In the oral phase, the infant's main preoccupation is food intake and pleasure is obtained through the mouth as a means of exploring the feeder's body. In the anal phase, bowel movements, potty-training and parental approval or disapproval become the focus for the organization of early sexual tendencies. In the **phallic** phase, the emphasis is placed on the expression of sexual feelings, primarily through masturbation.

In the genital phase, finally, sexuality is supposed to take the form of a mature relationship between adults, and sexual gratification is part of a more general feeling of well-being and satisfaction.

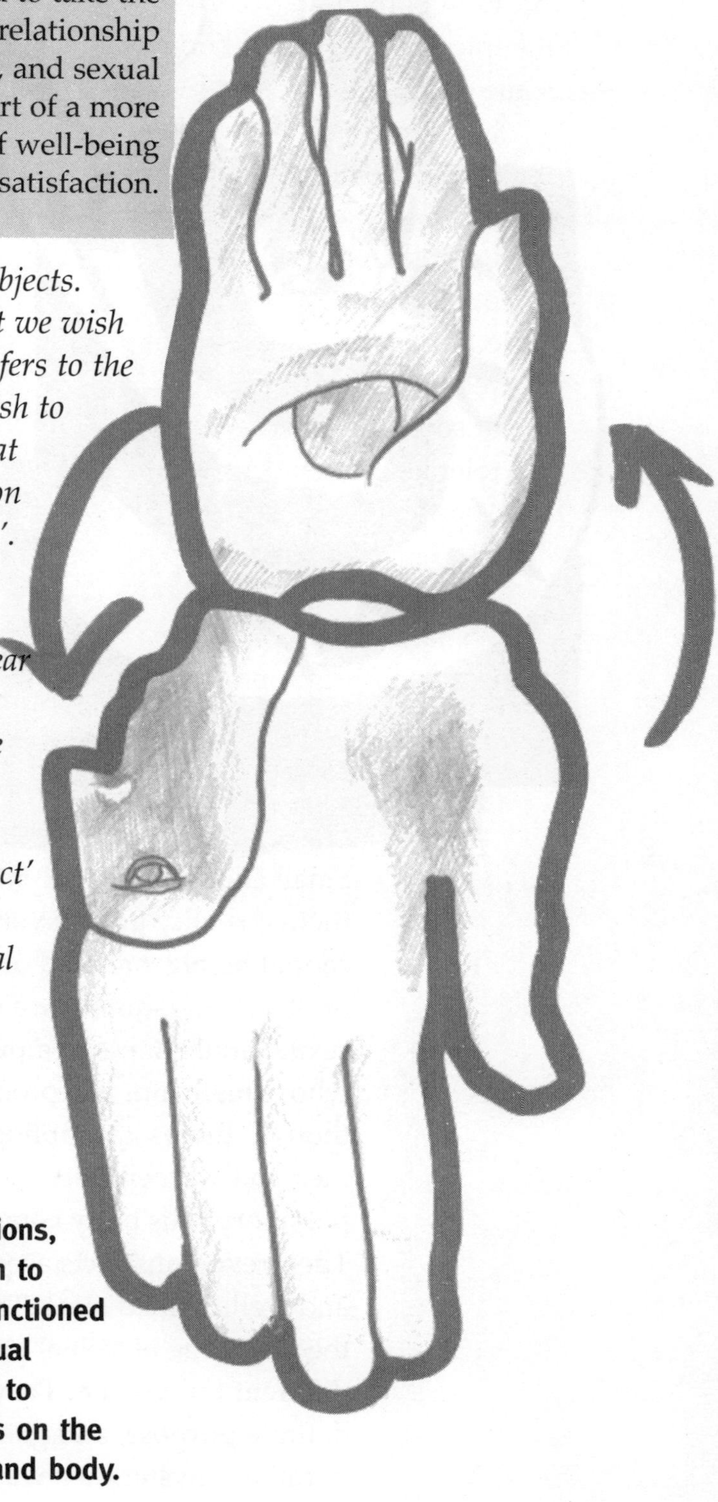

Sexuality has aims and objects. The 'aim' refers to the act we wish to perform; the 'object' refers to the person with whom we wish to perform it. Freud said that perversion is an aberration related to the sexual 'aim'. For example, if we derive more sexual pleasure from a partner's underwear than from her/his actual body, we 'suffer' from the perversion known as fetishism. The aberration related to the sexual 'object' is inversion. Freud saw homosexuality as a typical example of inversion, because the homosexual's object of desire doesn't conform to the 'norm'.

In perversions and inversions, sexual instincts may seem to deviate from culturally sanctioned expectations. But the sexual instinct is always difficult to categorize because it lives on the threshold between mind and body.

Small children are 'polymorphously perverse': their sexuality takes a variety of forms which cannot be pigeonholed on the basis of clear aims or objects. Gradually, we move from infantile sexual aimlessness to a purposeful adult sexuality whose main aim is reproduction. Here Freudian thought draws a troubling distinction between men and women. Men, apparently, leave the polymorphous body completely behind. Their sexual instincts acquire a clear direction and well-defined aims. Their guiding purpose is the discharge of sexual products. But things are different for women. They don't have such a definite purpose, and gain sexual satisfaction in rather 'mysterious' ways.

Female instinct retains traits of the infant's polymorphously perverse body. Freud's views on the subject of sexual instincts have done much to emplace the image of women's sexuality as ambiguous and enigmatic. The female body becomes a threat to the boundaries erected by the male sexual economy.

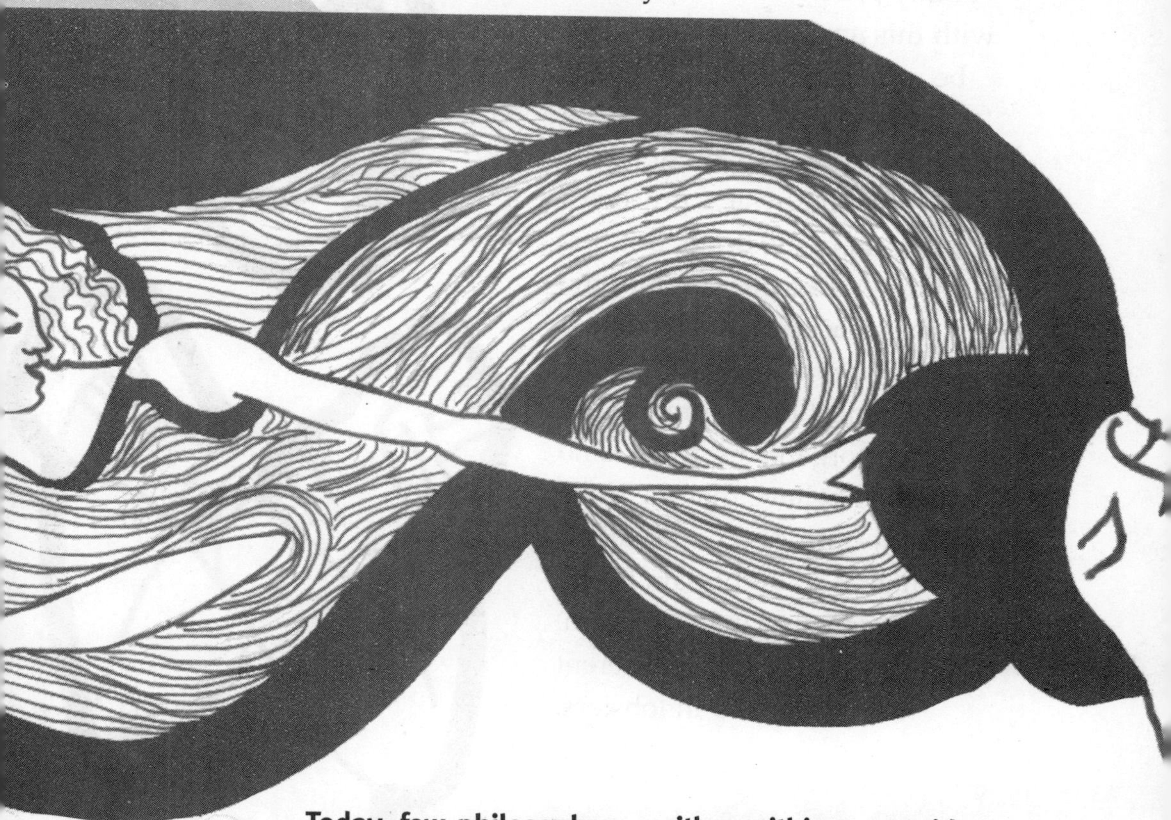

Today, few philosophers - either within or outside the field of psychoanalysis - would claim that we can function as pure **minds. Modern approaches to the mind-body issue suggest that the world as a whole is fundamentally** physical: **we can only get a grasp of ourselves, other people, animals and objects as bodies. If all matter were somehow removed from the world, there would be nothing left. Mental processes always take place within physical systems, such as biological bodies or organisms, not in some 'ghostly' immaterial being.**

The philosophical trend known as **physicalism** argues that the world should be studied primarily in terms of its physical laws. Our mental states are wholly dependent on bodily processes. The problem with this approach is that it can be rather reductive. We could say, for example, that the mental state of 'pain' depends on certain physical processes going on in the brain. But this doesn't take into account the fact that there are countless ways of experiencing pain, amongst both humans and other organisms: there is no reason to believe that the same physical process underlies all mental states of pain for all organisms capable of pain. Pain is probably very different in humans and in lobsters.

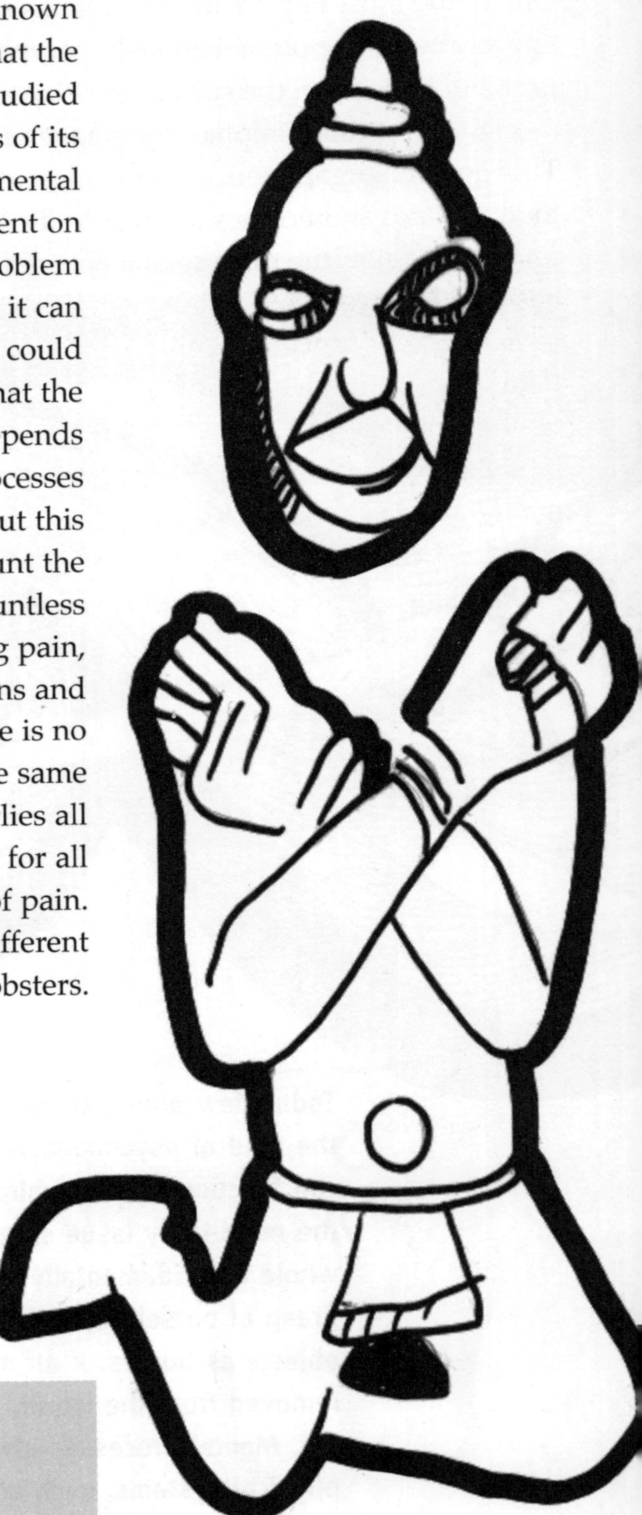

One of the most influential approaches to the mind-body problem in contemporary thought is **functionalism**. This position argues that mental states should be understood not in terms of basic bodily processes, but in terms of their 'functions'. Pain is a function which links up the physical experience of receiving damage and the mental state of desiring to get rid of it. Unlike physicalists, functionalists believe that it is impossible to identify mental states with fixed physical properties, because mental states can take a puzzling variety of forms.

One of the most important insights supplied by contemporary thought is that we acquire knowledge through the body.

From the earliest age, we learn through the body - both our own bodies and other people's. One of the hardest things to learn is what can and what cannot change in an object or in a body. Consider this basic example. A grown-up looks at a ball from one yard away in full daylight and registers one impression; s/he moves backwards shortly afterwards and sees something quite different; s/he then looks at the ball again in twilight and perceives something different still. The appearance of the ball has changed at least three times, but the adult observer knows that these transformations have to do with place and light, not with the ball itself. A small child doesn't know this. Every time s/he looks at the ball in different circumstances, s/he may well believe that the ball has become a different object.

It is by gradually becoming aware that our bodies are **separate** *from the outside world and that they don't change substantially when they move about, that we also learn that other objects and other people's bodies retain some kind of stability even if they look different, depending on their location.*

Small children learn to cope with their environment by adjusting their movements, postures and expressions to what they see around them. They often do this by imitating older people. Imitation helps children relate to others without direct physical contact. This is the first step towards learning that things exist even if they cannot be **touched**. This idea is later extended to the understanding that things exist even if they cannot be **seen**, especially in the case of other people's thoughts.

But children are not necessarily aware that they are adjusting themselves to their surroundings by means of their bodies. They follow what philosophers call a ***body schema****: a practical and nonconscious attunement to their environment. This happens before children are actually aware of* ***owning*** *a body.*

At a later stage, we find out that our bodies can perform acts intentionally and that these acts can affect other people's thoughts and feelings. At this point, we are no longer following a body schema but a **body image**. We are conscious of our bodies and of their actions. It would be incorrect to say that the body schema is peculiar to childhood and the body image to adulthood. Both are present in adult life. Whether we follow a body schema or a body image depends on the extent to which we act nonconsciously and instinctively, or consciously and intentionally.

The difference between body schema and body image can described through simple examples. If you raise your hand to wave at a friend or ask permission to speak, you doing so ***intentionally*** *(body image). If you shift your posture to maintain your balance when you're standing in a bus, you are doing so* ***automatically*** *(body schema). If you are suffering from eyestrain while reading, you may squint and move your face closer to the page quite unselfconsciously (body schema); or you may get up, turn on the light and put on your spectacles (body image)*

In any case, our bodies exist along with their environment. There are two ways of describing this connection. Some believe that as infants we don't think of ourselves as separate from our surroundings but only do this when we learn to move independently. Others believe that even tiny bodies have ways of distinguishing themselves from the outside world. Close observation of the newborn shows that they move their mouths, hands and eyes in fairly **organized** ways (to indicate hunger, pain, etc.) and that these movements are intentional rather than purely mechanical.

Influential work on the body image was carried out in the 1930s by Paul Schilder. He argued that the image of the body and the image of the world are hard to separate because there is an indeterminate zone between them. Neither image is natural.

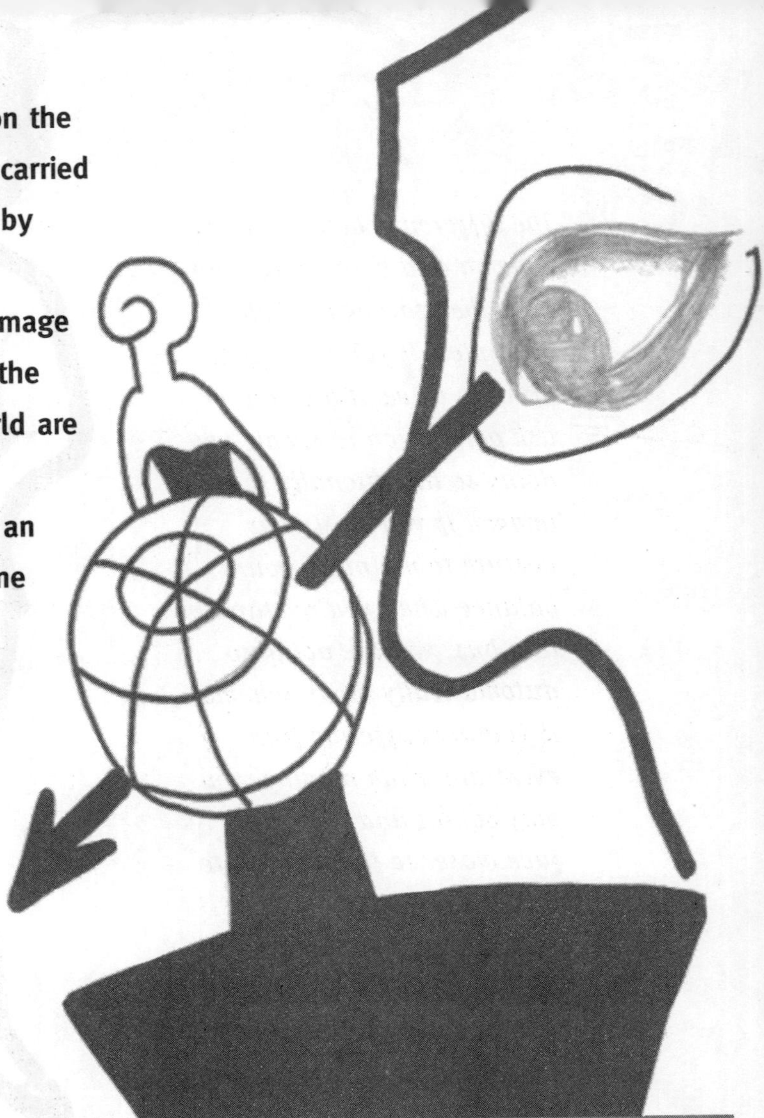

Both are constructed by the relationship between an individual's perceptions and her/his emotional and libidinal life. (The term **libido** as used by Freudian psychoanalysis refers specifically to sexual energies, but it can also be used to refer more generally to all the energies employed in the service of the life instinct, self-preservation and reproduction.)

For Schilder, body and body image are not necessarily the same thing. Breath, voice, blood and semen, for example, spill out of the body to the point that they become separate from it. Yet they are very much a part of the body image.

The body image also includes the space which surrounds the body. Any one body can produce different body images depending on the distance it places between itself and other bodies. If we're talking to strangers. or even to people we're acquainted with in a formal situation, we'll probably establish a certain amount of **contact-free** space between our bodies and theirs.

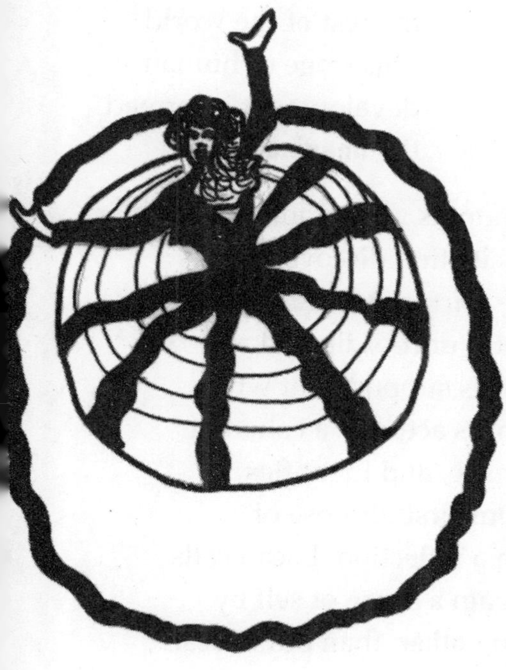

The size of this area would be substantially reduced in the company of a close friend, a lover or a pet. And then, of course, there are cases of enforced proximity - jam packed underground trains, football crowds, political demonstrations - where we may struggle to retain some imaginary distance between ourselves and others, whether or not this is actually viable.

One of the most intriguing interpretations of the relationship between the body and its environment can be found in the writings of the French psychoanalyst **Jacques Lacan (1901-81).** He argues that infants live in a state of **undifferentiation:** they do not experience their bodies as separate from the rest of the world. This stage of human development is termed the **Imaginary.**

Between six to eighteen months, the infant enters the **mirror phase:** it makes its first discovery of its body as a reflection in the mirror. At this early age, the infant's body is still uncoordinated and dependent on other people's support. But what the baby sees in the mirror is actually a coherent and autonomous body image, and identifies enthusiastically with it. Our first glimpse of identity is borrowed from a reflection. Lacan calls this a **misrecognition**: we gain a sense of self by identifying with something **other** than ourselves. We take the image to be our real body.

The next crucial shift takes place when we acquire language. Language plays a vital part in Lacan's theories. He argues that our understanding of our bodies and physical surroundings is **shaped by language.** What he means by 'language' is not simply words but rather all the **symbols** and **structures** that constitute a particular culture: social codes, conventions, laws, institutions, structures of kinship and gender roles. We can only function in the adult world if we have a grip on basic symbols shared by enough people to make communication possible. The **Symbolic Order** is the world we enter when we acquire language. In the Symbolic, we realize that our bodies are distinct from other people and objects.

In acquiring language, we also develop an **unconscious.** Lacan states that 'the unconscious is structured as a language'. This means that like language, the unconscious is made up of symbols and signs. But it also means that language **produces** the unconscious. When we acquire language, we have to adapt our desires and fantasies to the symbols which form the language of our culture. These symbols are always **limited:** they can never fully express all our fantasies and desires. What language cannot communicate must be repressed, pushed back beyond the level of consciousness. The **repressed** materials go to constitute the unconscious.

From this point onwards, human life is governed by an insatiable desire: the longing to make language **mean** what we wish to say, in the painful awareness that words can never fully embody the contents of our minds.

Often, we become the victims of another form of **misrecognition:** we assume we are in control of words and meanings, when in fact we are moulded by them. We do not speak language, we are **spoken by it.**

Before the acquisition of language, we don't know what to make of our bodies because we have no points of cultural reference outside ourselves. We cannot **define** our bodies. With language come ways of defining our bodies as separate.

We are given means to distinguish our bodies from the rest of the world. But the moment the body is framed by words, it, too, becomes a word, an **arbitrary cultural symbol.** In the Imaginary, the body is physical but cannot be defined. In the Symbolic, the body can be defined but is stripped of its materiality.

philosophical approaches

Empiricism and idealism are two of the most influential positions in Western philosophy. Their attitudes to the body differ substantially. But both relegate the body to a Cinderella-like position.

For the empiricists, the body is fundamentally **passive**: its only role is to register sensations caused by external objects. It is a combination of molecules which react to the impact of other objects according to the law of cause-and-effect. For the idealists, the most vital aspect of a human being is the mental or spiritual self. The self is all-powerful: it actually 'creates' the outside world by perceiving it. The body is simply the self's material **extension**, a secondary aspect of human life.

By figuring the body as a totally passive apparatus, empiricism robs it of any creative faculties. Idealism, for its part, subordinates the physical being to a disembodied consciousness.

Phenomenology and **existentialism** offer alternative approaches to the body. The body is not passive, because the world as we know it depends on the ways in which our bodies perceive it. Human consciousness is always caught up in the ebb and flow of material existence.

The term 'phenomenology' comes from the Greek word phenomenon: 'appearance', or how something 'manifests itself' to the senses and to the mind.

Phenomenology was initially associated with the writings of **Edmund Husserl (1859-1938).** Husserl was suspicious of physical experience because he saw it as far too subjective and personal. He was concerned with the logical patterns of thought which help us grasp the **universal** qualities of objects, and believed that the body could only perceive **particular** features.

The phenomenological thinker ***Martin Heidegger (1889-1976)*** *argued that mind and body cannot be separated. The world is a product of our mental projections: what we 'make' of it. But we are also physically subjected to the world: we are* ***flung down*** *or* ***thrown*** *into being, in a place and time we did not choose. We are both inside and outside nature. We have a will and a consciousness but we are also animals and therefore cannot adopt a stance of detached contemplation from a mountain top.*

Being, for Heidegger, has no fixed nature and can never be taken for granted. It is not a 'given' but a process of constant production. It has to be invented and reinvented at all times. This position anticipates the philosophical movement known as Existentialism.

Existentialism can be traced back to the writings of the Danish philosopher ***Søren Kierkegaard (1813-55).*** *He maintained that we are dominated by the image of an omnipotent God whose infinity reminds us all the time of our own flimsiness and absurdity - as* ***both bodies and minds.*** *'Angst' (dread, anxiety, anguish) is the governing principle of human life. Our destinies are never 'planned': we construct our lives* ***as we go along.*** *We only become individuals by making constant choices and commitments.*

This idea was later developed by the existentialist philosopher ***Jean-Paul Sartre (1905-80)****, who stated that 'existence precedes essence'. We come into being through the constant performance of choices and actions: 'man is only what he makes of himself'.*

Existence is the performance of a ritual comparable to the daily exercise taken by monks or prison inmates: a circular and repetitive experience. But this doesn't mean that it is predictable.

In fact, it is arbitrary and unmotivated or, as Sartre puts it, ***absurd****. Its repetitiveness and circularity suggest that it goes everywhere and nowhere at once.*

The famous lithograph titled ***Ascending and Descending*** *by* <u>*Maurits Cornelis Escher (1898-1972)*</u> *illustrates this concept of existence effectively. In the picture, a number of hooded figures walk around the upper courtyard of a building which could well be a prison or a monastery. It seems that they may be walking either clockwise or anticlockwise up the stairs or down: the exercise in which they are engaged is utterly pointless. Yet they pursue it relentlessly.*

Saying that Being is not fixed but impermanent is also a way of saying that human existence is unthinkable in separation from the body, for the body's very nature is one of continuous flux and change.

In certain strands of existentialist thought, the body comes to play a vital role in representing and experiencing the world. For **Maurice Merleau-Ponty (1907-61),** the form of an object depends on how the body perceives it, however erroneously and haphazardly. A key idea in Merleau-Ponty's theories is that of **embodiment.** By this he meant that we never perceive the world as pure consciousnesses. Consciousness is always embroiled in a tissue of flesh and blood.

The body is primarily a way of being in the world. It is a form of lived experience which is fluid and ever-shifting. And it is also a way of interacting with one's environment, of shaping it and being shaped by it.

This experience can be simply dismissed as a pathetic illusion, of course. But it also shows that we do not only relate to our bodies as material substances. We also have a sense, however hazy, of physical possibilities which are not materially available and present. The experience of a phantom limb is a reaching out of the body from real modes of being into **potential** modes of being. It points to something which our bodies no longer are, but it also points to what our bodies are not **yet**, and could therefore become. Merleau-Ponty's body is a space of virtual identities.

According to Merleau-Ponty, we do not only relate to our environment through the **present** body but also through the **absent** body. He talks, in particular, of the 'phantom limb' - the phenomenon whereby people can go on experiencing the presence of a part of their body after it has been amputated.

There is a parallel between this approach and certain positions in the field of **sociobiology.** Some scientists argue that bodily and mental states are programmed according to the environment we inhabit. But patterns of thought and action produced by the environment do not exhaust human potentialities. The energies which are not 'used up' by the contingent environment are retained, subliminally, and may be activated in a different environment. This view is quite refreshing, because it assumes that although we are necessarily conditioned by the context in which we live, we also have the power to imagine and fashion alternative realities.

a history of the body?

Does the body have a history? Or does it borrow a history from whatever discipline happens to be studying it? Is the body's history a history of art? of science? of language? of ideas?

A fairly new approach to the body sees it as the point of convergence of ***many histories,*** *rather than the object of a singular investigation. The phrase 'history of the body' is increasingly used to describe changing views on the body in relation to several fields of study: medicine, technology, art, literature, law, education, food, fashion, gender and labour.*

The most important contribution to this patchwork history comes from the writings of **Michel Foucault (1926-84).** For Foucault, the body is central to the **social sciences** (psychology, medicine, sociology, criminology) and to the **institutions** through which such sciences operate (hospitals, schools, prisons, law courts). Both the human sciences and institutions work according to one main rule: **defining the difference** between **'normal'** and **'abnormal'** bodies. Once this distinction is established, people's behaviour can be regulated and disciplined.

But there are no unchanging criteria for deciding what is aberrant. Perceptions of madness, sickness, disability and criminality, for instance, alter radically over time. One thing is fairly constant, though: we don't define the abnormal through the normal but vice versa. In other words, we don't decide that a certain kind of body is legitimate and then go on to decide that other kinds of bodies are unacceptable by contrast. We work the other way round. We single out abnormality and then determine what normality should be. This means that we look out obsessively for signs of the abnormal body, because without an idea of the abnormal we could have no idea of the normal. Abnormality is necessary to our sense of identity.

'Improper' bodies are excluded from society in many ways. But no 'proper' body could ever function without them. If all abnormal bodies were magically to be made normal, the very concept of normality would disappear - and with it , the idea of an **authorized** social identity would vanish as well. Although definitions of the abnormal body change over time, its cultural role doesn't. Societies have to go on incessantly spotting new forms of deviation from the norm in order to formulate up-to-date versions of normality.

*The definition of the **insane** body is of special interest for Foucault. The mentally sick are confined and hidden away in cultures where madness is regarded as shameful. In pre-modern societies, it was quite common for so-called **lunatics** to inhabit the same social space as the mentally healthy. Ominously, when segregation was introduced, mad people were relegated to the asylums once used to keep **lepers** out of sight.*
*By banishing the insane body, society doesn't aim at **curing** it but rather at setting up an image of anomalous behaviour against which sanity can be asserted.*

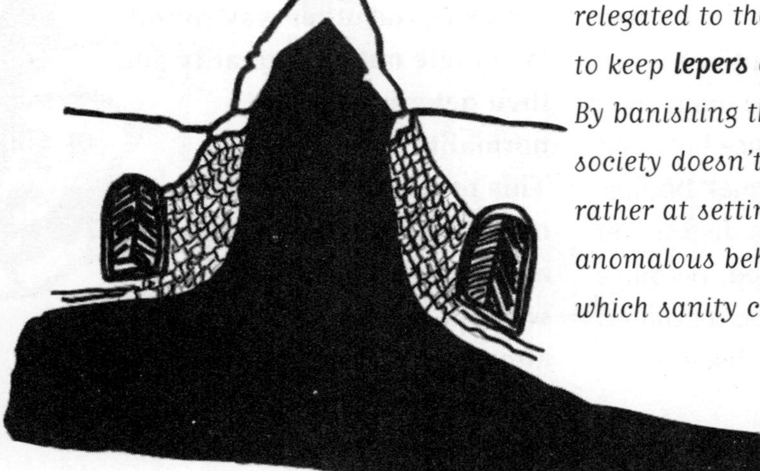

The body is controlled through **dividing practices,** designed to segregate the sick, the insane and the unlawful. To begin with, law and order relied on the public display of pain (e.g. through torture) and on the spectacle of execution as powerful deterrents. But in the eighteenth century, with the development of the modern penal system, imprisonment became the single form of punishment for all crimes. At the same time, the prison system began to supply a model for other institutions: schools, armies, hospitals, factories. All these structures, like the prison, are based on similar disciplinary mechanisms: each body has its appointed place in the system; all activities are controlled by strict timetables; repetitive exercises must be regularly performed; inflexible hierarchies must be respected.

The shift from a culture of spectacle to a culture of imprisonment affected deeply people's ways of seeing the world. For Foucault, power always relies on the eye.

In pre-modern societies, the powerful advertized their authority by putting themselves on display (think of royal processions, for example) and awing the powerless masses into submission.

In modern societies, power has become **invisible:** it sees everything while remaining unseen. Power relies on an all-seeing **gaze.** Our culture is

based on the idea of the **Panopticon:** an ideal prison in which each body is confined to a small cell and can be observed all the time by a single person sitting in a central tower. The inmates can be seen constantly but cannot see either their observer or one another. This same structure can apply to schools, hospitals, factories and barracks. *(More will be said about Foucault's views on the gaze in the section on* ***The Body and the Visual.****)*

The gaze also plays a vital role in the medical field. Classical approaches to the body were based mainly on ***external*** *analysis and were concerned with the surfaces of the body from an anatomical point of view. Modern medicine is based on corporeal penetration. It aims at regulating the body's* ***inner*** *functionings. Autopsies enabled medicine to subject the entire body, not just its surfaces, to the power of the scientific gaze. The doctor's power was no longer associated with his theoretical knowledge but rather with his way of seeing the body, probing and scrutinizing it down to the tiniest detail.*

In modern societies, each of the body's drives is thoroughly manipulated for the purpose of producing efficient and 'docile' subjects. The sense that we are being looked at all the time supports this process. We are made to think that we have to control our bodies so that they will appear normal and respectable to our invisible observer. We are made to feel ashamed and guilty if we fail to conform to what is acceptable.

Philosophy argued for centuries that 'the body is the prison of the soul'. The body was seen as a flimsy and transient shell from which the immortal soul longed to escape. Foucault maintains that, in fact, the soul is the prison of the body. The body is enslaved to abstract principles of propriety and usefulness. These principles are the 'soul' which culture imposes on us.

We always perceive the world as bodies and this means that our perceptions are inevitably distorted. This should not, however, lead to despair: there is much pleasure to be derived from the experience of distortion.

If we look through the water in a pool at the tiles at the bottom of the pool, the tiles do not look as they really are, for they are distorted by ripples of sunlight, reflections and refractions. Similarly, if we look at a landscape through a stained glass window, we do not see the landscape as it really is: it is transformed by the colours and shapes of the window's pattern. In both cases, the media through which we look (water and glass) inevitably **misrepresent** the actual things we are looking at. **But they also make things pleasing in unexpected ways.**

The images of the world we obtain and create through our bodies are necessarily distorted. But this doesn't mean we should blame the body for misconstruing reality. Distortion is not a secondary or accidental aspect of human experience. We never see the world as it is. We only ever perceive it through various 'filters' and 'channels'.

*Our images of the world are not **slices of life,** cut out of a stable reality ordained by the gods. They are **constructions**, or artificial organizations of meaning. Neither the body nor the mind 'reflect' reality. Rather, they **represent** it according to both conscious and unconscious codes and conventions.*

Western culture has traditionally been unwilling to admit either that there is no reality free of distortion or that all images of the world are constructed. This is because our way of thinking has been dominated by Realism. Realism wants to hide the fact that our images of the world are constructed. It would rather have us think that images mirror reality, that they offer a keyhole view on a solid world, there for everyone to share. Realism maintains that reality can be grasped objectively and neutrally. This is a powerful ideological ploy. It tells us that reality is unchanging, for to deny that something was made is to deny that it could ever be unmade, disputed or undermined. Realism fosters the principle of ideological stability. But once we accept that all images of the world are cultural fabrications, we begin to realize that if an image can be assembled, it can also be disassembled.

Objectivity is a myth designed to make us believe that there is one correct way of seeing and representing reality - and therefore a means of marginalizing all that is different, other, alternative. The myth of objectivity can be undermined by distorting deliberately certain familiar images and showing that distortion doesn't erase reality but actually makes it more real. Non-realistic representations can tell us important things about people and their bodies. They often have a greater impact on our senses than realistic images do, because they can avail themselves of a wider range of techniques and tools.

For example, photography can employ all sorts of 'tricks' to produce bodies that look quite unreal by naturalistic standards and yet convey ***very*** *real ways of thinking about the body. Photography's bodies can be pieced together from fragments of reproductions of famous images or anatomical representations.*

*They can be drained of all volume and solidity, made to look like dummies, have bits of animal bodies grafted onto them. Minor physical blemishes such as scars, moles and birthmarks can be magnified to grotesque proportions. The body can be looked at from such unfamiliar angles that familiar shapes such as arms and legs become totally disorienting. In other words, photography can **edit** the body through all sorts of chemical, optical and electronic devices to the point that the body becomes almost unrecognizable. But this doesn't relegate the body to the province of sheer fantasy.*

The surreal hallucinations produced by photographic editing are actually accurate representations of deep-seated fantasies, anxieties and fears. 'Real' bodies are, after all, culturally fashioned on the models supplied by famous images. They are, often, materially shrunk, turned into dolls, animals, or disturbing hybrids. So-called unrealistic techniques make us aware that processes of bodily construction are in operation at all times.

***Digital photography** has complicated further the relationship between reality and its representations. Critics who believe in the traditional aims and objectives of Realism - its ability to mirror reality accurately and without distortions - find it quite scandalous that photographs should be 'tampered with' by means of computer assisted techniques. What they find especially disturbing about these practices is not their application in general terms, but rather their specific application to the medium of photography. This is because photography is conventionally held to be the most truthful and reliable way of documenting the world. Photography is often seen as synonymous with the 'documentary'.*

Yet any photograph, much as it may try to document reality dispassionately, results from individual choices of subject matter and perspective, processes of selection, framing, focusing, etc. Digital photography, as other arts keen on playing with virtual reality, reminds us that the world is not a real space but rather the ***reconstruction of an illusion of real space.*** *The more we* ***experiment*** *with reality, the more we open reality up and discover new procedures for constructing it.*

Contemporary perspectives on the relationship between the body and the world emphasize that reality is only ever *what we make of it,* an effect of how we read it and depict it through the lenses of private and public fantasies. It is by coming to terms with the inevitability of distortion that we may begin to understand how endlessly fascinating reality could be. After all, despite our attempts to delimit and explain our dreams, the fact remains that we go on dreaming.

the body in the visual Field

Outline

The body is shaped by how we see it and represent it. We are culturally trained to perceive the body in organized ways, from certain angles and through certain lenses. Vision is always socially groomed. A culture's power structures depend largely on how we look and are looked at.

power and the eye

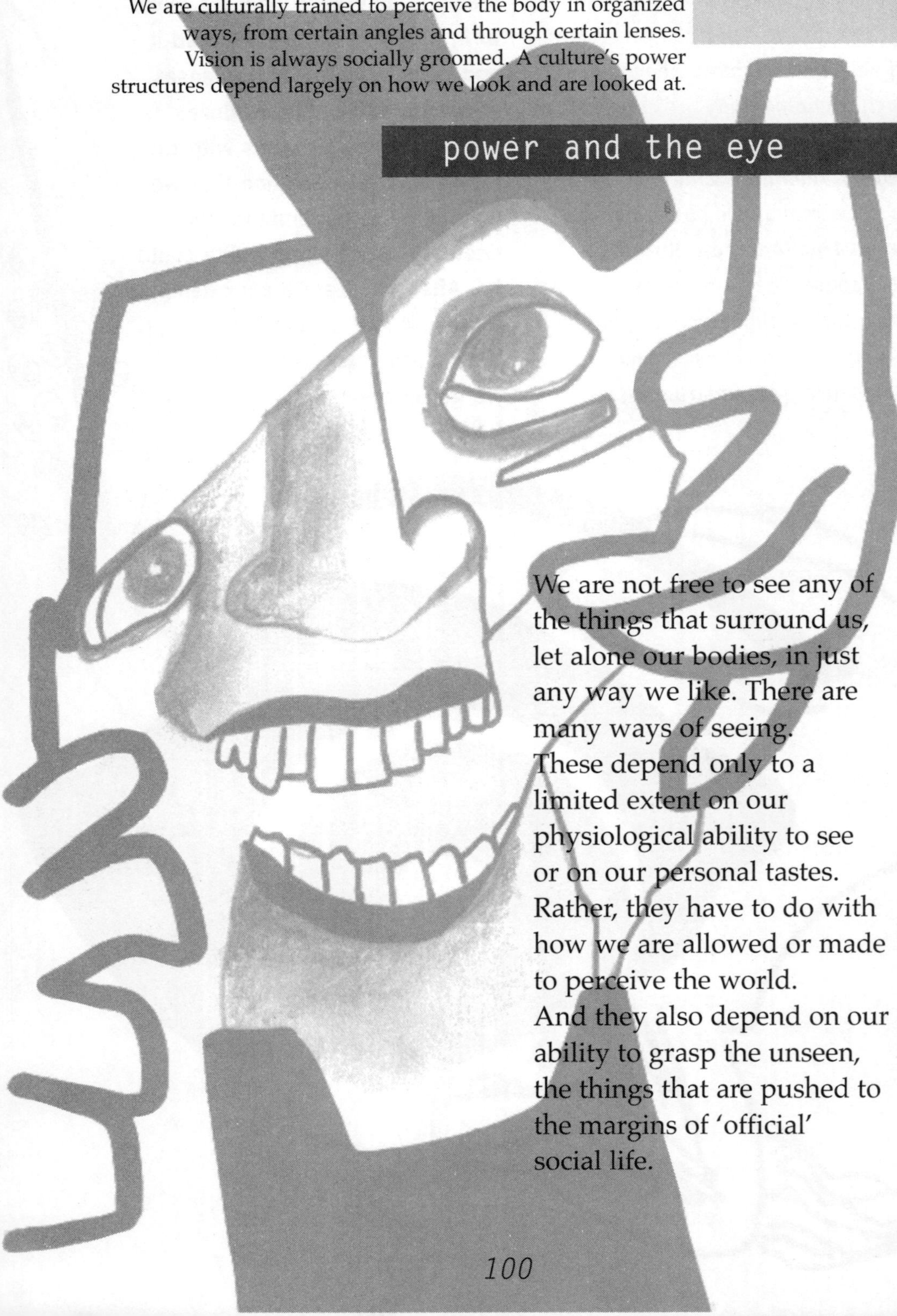

We are not free to see any of the things that surround us, let alone our bodies, in just any way we like. There are many ways of seeing. These depend only to a limited extent on our physiological ability to see or on our personal tastes. Rather, they have to do with how we are allowed or made to perceive the world. And they also depend on our ability to grasp the unseen, the things that are pushed to the margins of 'official' social life.

When we see things, we are not necessarily looking at them. And when we look at things, we may act as spectators or as observers. A spectator is basically an onlooker. An observer is somebody who doesn't simply look at the world but actually perceives it according to specific rules. 'To observe' means to comply with or to conform to certain rules and regulations. All visual forms of expression involve particular guidelines, procedures and laws. In abiding to such principles, we fashion our bodies in culturally approved ways.

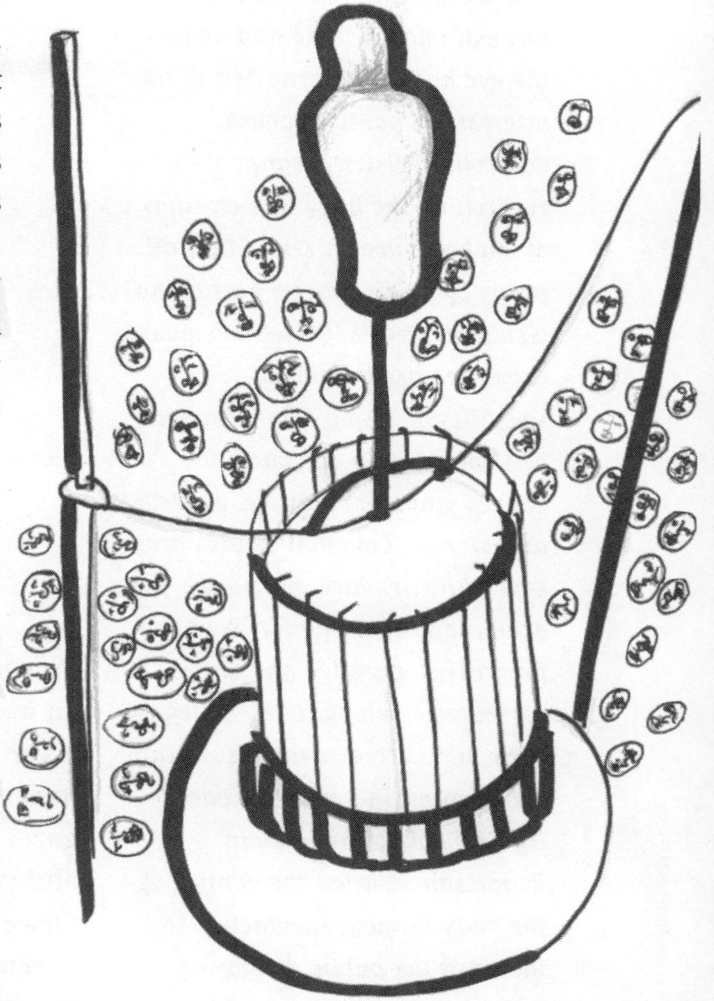

Painting, photography and cinema are not merely media or techniques but rather ways of constructing the body through images. Cinema, for example, is not just a mechanical apparatus made of cameras and projectors but also a means of giving form to our fantasies and fears. A slasher is often chilling because it reminds us of our bodies' vulnerability; a romance is often titillating because it expresses erotic longings.

Many cultural factors determine how we see and represent the body through images. Time and again, the eye has been harnessed to the interests of political power. Controlling vision means controlling the body. The writings of Michel Foucault stress that all forms of power rely on particular visual strategies. Sometimes power expresses itself through sensational display. The body can be turned into a spectacle to convey glamour, prestige, expertise and status. 'Common' bodies are kept 'in their place' by lavish exhibitions of authority. Royal progresses, parades and state ceremonies belong to this category. Their aim is to awe the viewer into submission. This practice can be traced back to the western Renaissance, when the control of the body through spectacle included the public display of torture and execution.

Power can also use the eye as an instrument of surveillance. It can dominate its subjects by means of an all-encompassing gaze, which sees everything and yet remains unseen. George Orwell capitalized on this idea in **Nineteen Eighty Four** through the mighty figure of 'Big Brother' and his omnipresent camera eyes. But power doesn't always gaze at us through specific individuals. Our society isn't neatly divided into two categories: those who watch and those who are watched. Our bodies are moulded by how they are seen. But most of the time we don't really know ***who is watching whom.***

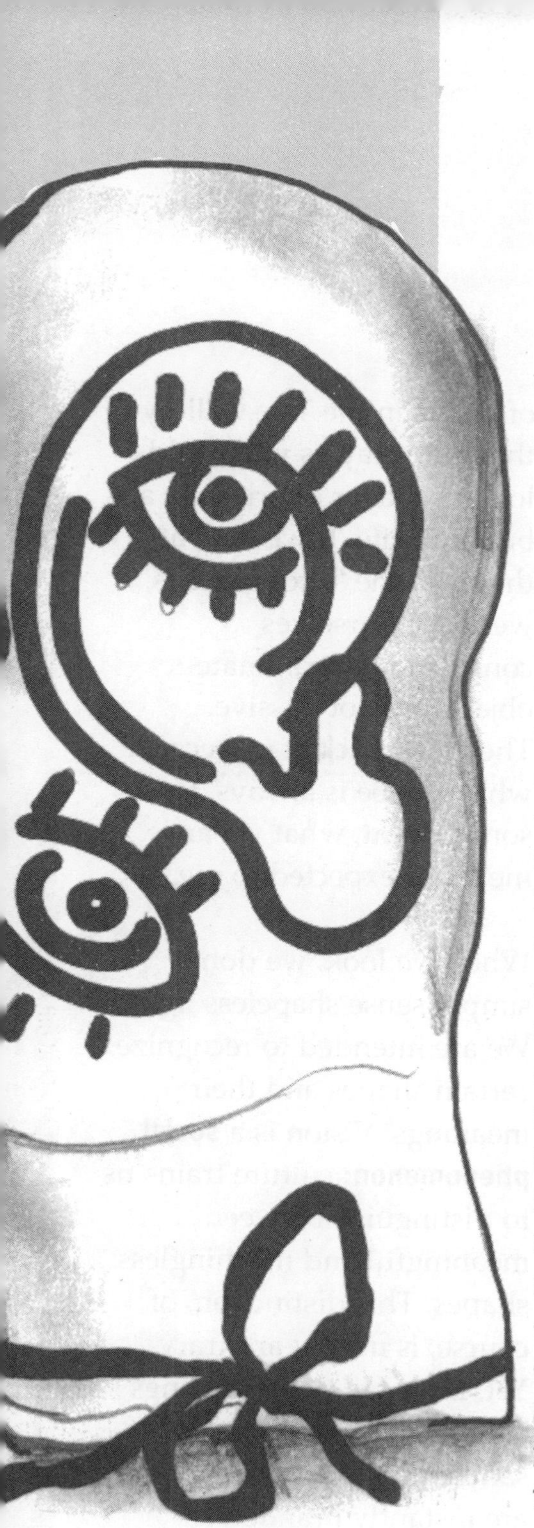

We can't single out a particular person or group of people and say: 'you are the power that is shaping me!' What actually happens is more devious and harder to recognize.

---

*Power **flows** through our society as an often invisible force. It cannot be instantly associated with a ruler or ruling party. The power that defines us by constantly gazing at our bodies is **everywhere**: in the form of moral and religious rules, legal systems and mass-produced images, for example. These laws and images **look at** us, even if no one particular human being can be spotted behind them, because they embody ideas of cultural acceptability. We know that when we fail to conform to those ideas, we become unacceptable (deviant, irregular, undesirable). Maybe nobody is literally watching us. But powerful ideas are there all the time to remind us what we should look like and how we should look at other people and objects. There comes a point when we become critical surveyors of ourselves. There's no need for Big Brother any more. Once we have **internalized** power's gaze, we are the first to know if we've stepped off the mark.*

Most of the images we see aim at telling us how we should behave and display ourselves. The external appearance of our bodies is supposed to communicate our inner worth (ethically, politically, sexually). We can't really behold anything without having to wonder what's **expected** of us.

If I look at another person in a certain way, what will that person (and the rest of the world) make of me? **Can I look at anybody else without having to worry about how** I **am being perceived? And the same goes for objects.**

Inanimate things don't literally look at us. But we know that we are meant to look at them in certain ways, depending on their contexts. For example, we are not supposed to perceive a layer of bricks in the Tate Gallery in the same way as we would look at a layer of bricks in a building site. If we look at things in the 'wrong' ways, we make ourselves conspicuous. Inanimate objects are not passive. They **look back** at us because what we see is always, to some extent, what we are meant or expected to see.

When we look, we don't simply sense shapeless light. We are intended to recognize certain shapes and their meanings. Vision is a **social phenomenon:** culture trains us to distinguish between meaningful and meaningless shapes. This distinction, of course, is utterly arbitrary. Yet, if we fail to view things according to socially sanctioned benchmarks, we are instantly branded as visually disturbed or as the victims of hallucination.

People have not seen things identically throughout history. Vision changes as political and economic circumstances do. Let's look at a couple of examples.

One. In the Renaissance, the philosophy of humanism preached that 'Man', not 'God', was at the centre of the universe. The invention of perspective backed up this idea. Perspective is a visual technique meant to make things look **as they really are.** It creates the illusion of depth on a two-dimensional surface, by representing bodies as larger or smaller depending on whether they are close up or far away. But it is something else, too. It is a way of controlling vision according to strict mathematical rules. Perspectivalism says that the human eye can dominate the world and that its gaze can be structured scientifically. Vision is not a haphazard event: it is calculated and measurable. There must be **one** correct way of seeing. To be truly objective, the eye should disregard the body and all the senses other than sight.

This aim is clearly unattainable. Vision is always partial. We always see things from a specific and therefore reductive angle: there is no neutral vantage point. Each of our two eyes, regardless of impairments, sees differently. What's more, we never see anything without, at the same time, being seen. We are always both subjects and objects of seeing. Sight is neither mathematically verifiable nor isolated from the rest of the body: when we see, our eyes perform in conjunction with the other senses. The idea of a disembodied eye is a spurious myth. But why should Renaissance artists and scientists be so eager to promote this myth?

A possible answer to this question is that perspective was born as a visual means of asserting human mastery in a historical context riddled with uncertainties and anxieties. The Renaissance was undoubtedly a time of momentous change.

Political and religious doctrines were radically quizzed; economic development and scientific progress forced people to reassess their place in the cosmos; the world, remapped by colonial expansion, was found to be much vaster and more mysterious than before; the whole universe was reconfigured and the body itself took a new form. Anatomy and perspective enabled artists to dissect and redesign the body and to represent figures with a weight and solidity unknown since Classical times.

This is a way of affirming the importance of physicality, of putting the imprint of western Man around the world as a commanding presence. But it is also a sign of uncertainty. Renaissance culture needed to represent the body in all its concreteness because it had to find ways of lending substance to a world eroded by scepticism and doubt.

Two. Another example of shifting patterns of seeing can be found in the nineteenth century. At that time, vision was deeply affected by the social multiplication of images: through geographical and colonial expansion, the wider distribution of illustrated papers, industrialization, and the technological development of new optical instruments.

People had more ways of seeing than before. This could help them feel more powerful. But it also took something away from them. Mechanical eyes could now take the place of human eyes and rob them of their traditional privileges. Machines could see for **people. The artificial body was beginning to haunt the biological one.**

With the growth of mechanical forms of vision, the bodily eye is decentred. It becomes just one tool out of many. Why spend ages trying to paint a body, object or landscape, when any of them can be photographed in instants? Some people believe that there is something uniquely creative about the amount of **labour** that goes into painting.

But surely, photography too is creative: the photographer must make imaginative decisions about the angle from which a picture is to be taken in order to achieve certain effects of light, pattern and perspective. Contemporary digital photography emphasizes, moreover, that a photograph is an endlessly **reworkable** representation. The invention of photography in 1839 was a healthy challenge for many painters. In the 1870s, several Impressionist 'masters' would draw inspiration from photographs.

What's more, we should not forget that there are crucial similarities between the eye and the camera...

the eye and the camera

A good photographer knows that to get a picture right the light intensity must be right. If the light is too dim, the picture will be 'underexposed'; if the light is too bright, the picture will be 'overexposed'. Cameras contain devices that can adjust the light received by the film to the appropriate level. The human eye functions similarly. It excludes or allows light to enter the body through the eyelids, the equivalent of the camera **shutter.**

The pupil, a variable opening, further regulates the amount of light that has been let in by shrinking or expanding.
*The pupil is comparable to the **aperture** of a camera. If a bright light is shone into the eye, the pupil narrows, to protect the retina from too intense illumination. Gradually, the retina adjusts to the level of light, and the pupil goes back to its initial size. In bright light, the pupil only has a two-millimetre diameter; in twilight, one of ten millimetres. But while light intensity can change over ten thousand times, the pupil area can only change up to twenty-five times. This goes to show that the eye is not all-powerful: we shouldn't always trust what we see!*

Despite the similarities, there is an important difference between the biological eye and the photographic camera. The camera **snaps** an image and fixes it permanently. The eye doesn't. It records images as scenes in constant movement. It uses different nerves and combines their messages in different ways to adapt to its surroundings. The retina, in particular, has two types of cells: **cones**, which work best in bright light, and **rods**, which we need to see in dim light. But this doesn't mean that the eye handles two 'films' simultaneously. What it means is that different signals interplay all the time. They are transmitted to the brain and here processed into a more or less coherent picture. ***This makes the human eye more like a TV camera than a photographic camera.***

Our limited ability to adjust to a phenomenon as crucial as illumination warns us against the temptation to rely unreservedly on the sense of sight. The realization that the eye deals not with frozen frames but with moving images challenges further the authority of seeing. We never see one **thing in** one **way. We are actually incessantly processing billions of visual impulses through various channels and codes. These codes are largely determined by a culture's ideological agendas. Western culture, specifically, has been governed by three main principles.**

One: *It has prioritized sight as the most reliable of the senses. Sight does not require physical proximity in the way the other senses, especially touch and smell, do. For this reason, it has been associated with the rational mind rather than the animal body.*

Two: *It has endeavoured to standardize sight by codifying scientifically correct ways of seeing (e.g. through perspective).*

Three: *It has used the sense of sight and the idea of regulated vision to* ***fix*** *the body.*

The eye/camera analogy can be employed to support this project.
It states: 'The camera sees you. It sees you objectively. It frames you.'
The comparison between the biological eye and the photographic camera is seductive because it suggests that the eye, too, could frame or fix reality.
But the realization that the eye resembles a TV camera more than a photographic one emphasizes that reality is not a sequence of frozen snapshots but rather a matter of ceaseless movement and flow.

We should also remember that no medium mirrors the world objectively. Any image and any instrument used to produce images derive their power from their ideological usefulness. Photography, in its basic form, constructs a world based on the triumph of light over darkness. It makes light the precondition of vision, the medium of action. This is a technical process, but it can also be turned into a world view: conventionally, light means enlightenment, truth, rationality, everything to do with the **mind,** whereas darkness means the unknown, basic instincts, the **body**. And of course, the battle between light and darkness also evokes sinister racial prejudices.

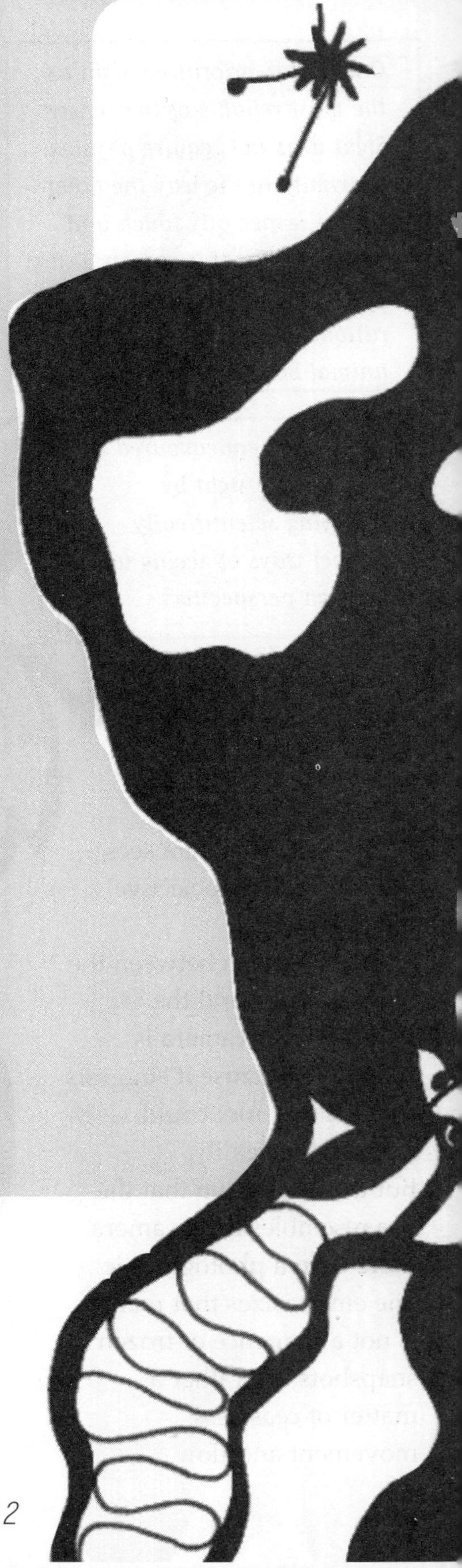

Digital photography, or **post-photography,** has complicated the game. Images have become increasingly malleable. It has become possible to change any detail of a photograph, no matter how small or large, by scanning the image on a computer screen and using a variety of tools to add or take away elements, alter colours, change the focus.

If in traditional photography the body is just the dark subject-matter of light-bearing technologies, in digital photography the body is an active maker and re-shaper of reality. Things are not there to be fixed but to be endlessly transformed. Bodies can be reinvented, distorted, collaged, dismembered or fictionalized. This shows that the body is not the theme of a frozen 'portrait' but something exuberantly alive, even once it has been placed into a frame.

A good example of the difference between conventional photography and digital photography can be found in Ridley Scott's **Blade Runner.** The replicant Rachael clings to a conventional photograph, a fake snapshot of a little girl she's never been and a mother she's never had, as evidence of her memory and a guarantee of her identity. Deckard, on the other hand, scans, enhances and comes close to entering a space where he could capture a fugitive replicant by digital means.

In contemporary culture, we are faced with the possibility that bodies may exist ***purely*** *as images, and that images may even appear more natural than the things themselves. Consider a classic example. King Kong was a solid model of an imaginary creature manipulated so as to look real. The dinosaurs in* ***Jurassic Park,*** *by contrast, are computer generated images. The gigantic ape is a concrete body, though artificial. The creatures in Spielberg's film are totally derealized bodies that never existed outside a computer. Which is more effective?*

What's more, there is evidence that digitally processed bodies can create surprisingly *solid* ***effects.*** *Who Framed Roger Rabbit?,* ***for instance, 'works' because it blends the figures, the toon and the man, with amazing naturalness thanks to computers.***

the gaze

The concept of the gaze describes a form of power associated with the eye and with the sense of sight. Certain bodies can wield power over other bodies by looking at them in certain ways. When we gaze at somebody or something, we are not simply 'looking'. The gaze probes and masters. It penetrates the body and bounds it as a passive object. **The gaze objectifies the body.**

A lot of the time, we simply 'see' things: we register certain sensations to do with light, colours and shapes without any ulterior motives. Sometimes we 'observe' things: we look at them carefully in order to find out about them in detail. Then there are times when we 'glance' at things: our eyes skim over them and caress their surfaces in a casual way, perhaps hoping for some unexpected surprise. But when we *gaze* at things, our aim is to control them.

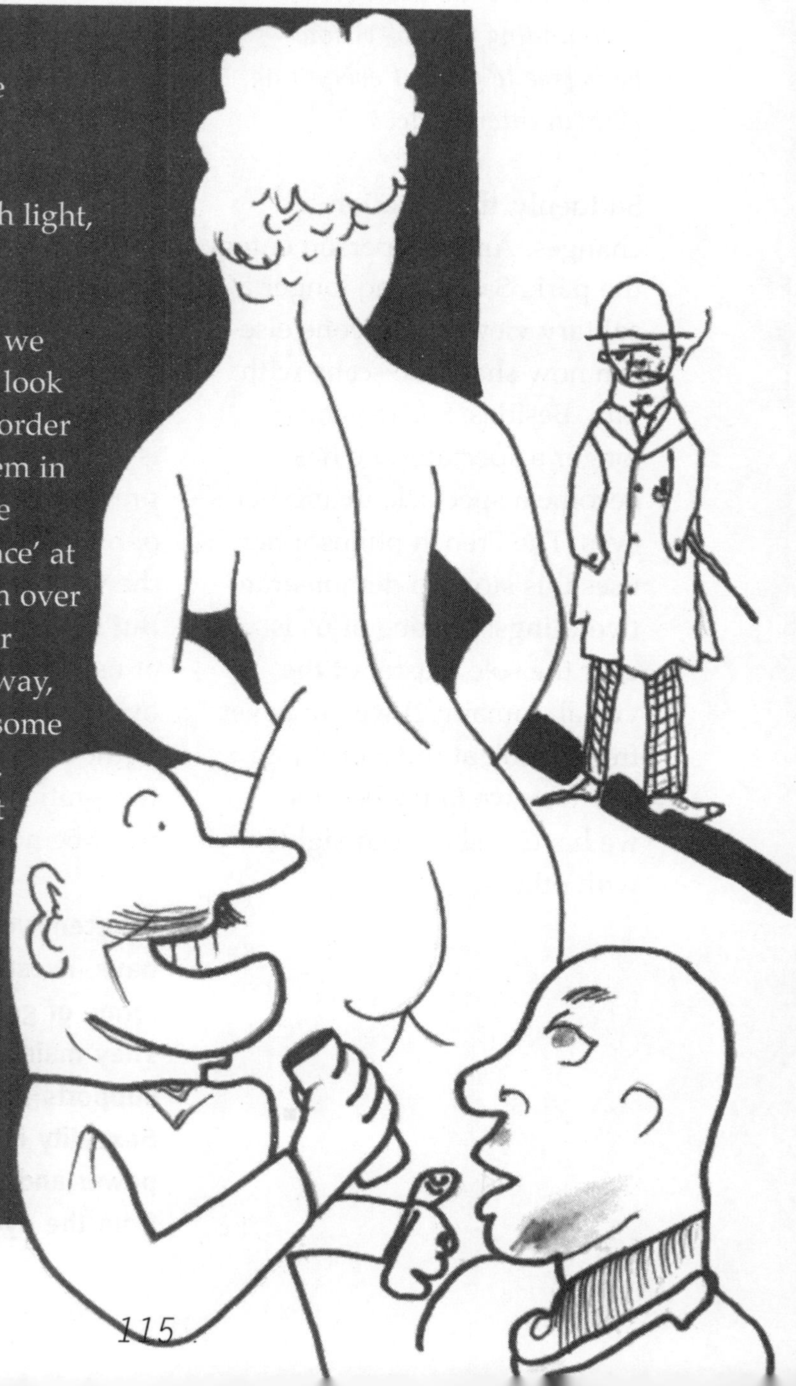

Jean-Paul Sartre argued that human identity is a product of the gaze. He explained this idea through a simple yet disturbing allegory. Sartre walks into a park; he notices that he is alone; he is pleased by the realization that he is the only one in control of the surrounding field of vision: he is free to gaze at everything without interferences.

Suddenly, the situation changes. Another person enters the park. Sartre is no longer a solitary viewer: someone else can now share the scene with him. Besides, Sartre is no longer a spectator: he has become a spectacle to another's eyes. The French philosopher uses this story to demonstrate two things: **1)** none of us is ever the sole master of the visual domain; **2)** we are never free to look at the world just any way we fancy because we have to share our sight with others.

These reflections lead Sartre to a third point: **3)** our sense of identity depends on the presence of another person. The person is an 'intruder' whose presence shatters our fantasies of unchallenged control of the visual world.
But the intruder, in gazing at us, also **recognizes** our existence. And for Sartre, without the other's recognition that we exist, we'd be nothing at all.

In recent years, several critics have investigated the gaze in terms of gender relations. They maintain that the gaze supports sexual power structures. Sexuality is inseparable from power and power is inseparable from the eye.

Laura Mulvey, for example, has discussed the role of the gaze in mainstream Hollywood cinema to argue that female characters in that tradition are controlled by the male gaze. The male protagonist objectifies the heroine through his gaze.

The male spectator identifies with the filmic hero and uses his own gaze to frame the heroine as a passive object. Objectification can take two forms. Both produce particular **stereotypes** of femininity.

***One.* Woman is** devalued **as a demon, a symbol of sexual corruption. The demonic woman fuels male fantasies of containment of the female body: she is the overpowering animal to be repressed.**

***Two.* Woman is** over-valued **as an artwork, a symbol of Platonic purity and beauty. The idealized woman reflects the male desire to transform the female body into a desexualized icon to be placed on a pedestal and worshipped from a distance.**

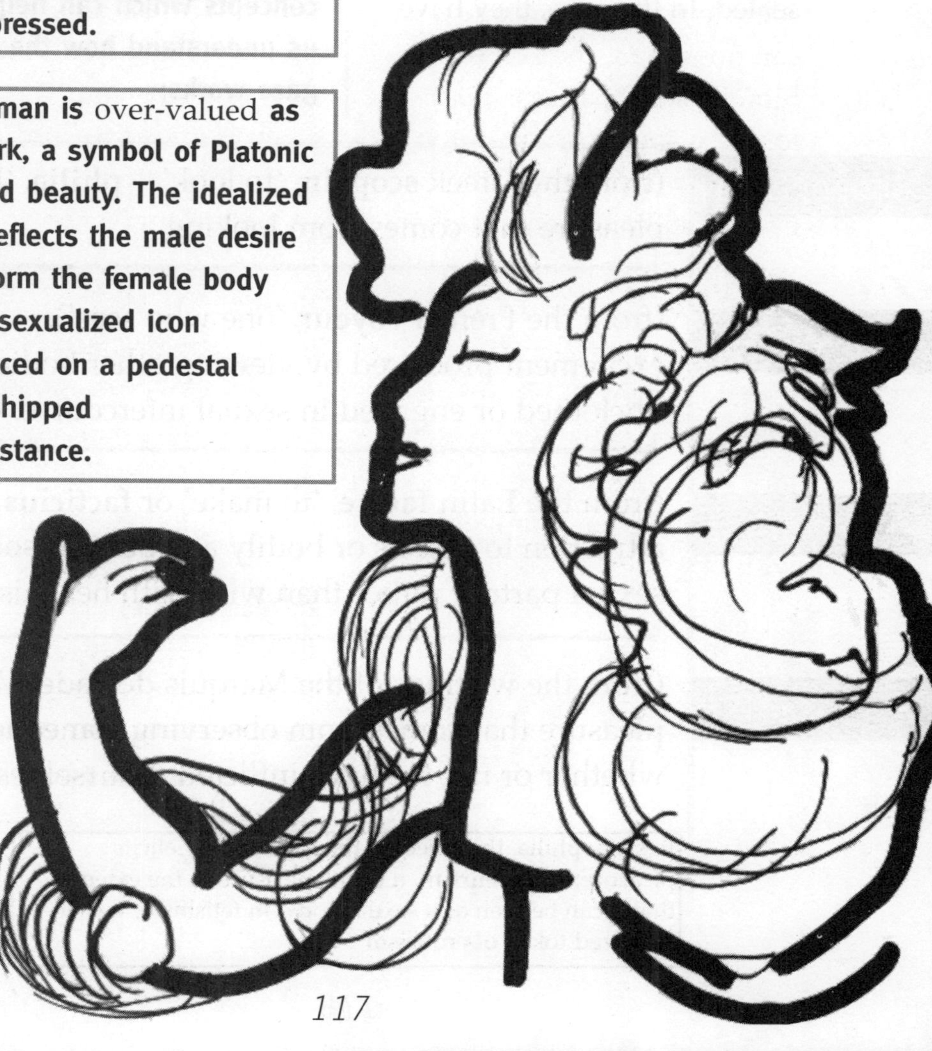

Lynda Nead makes similar points in her study of the female nude in western art. Traditionally, the female body has been found 'disturbing' because of its lack of clear boundaries. It's been seen as leaky and messy, and its boundlessness has been associated with female sexuality as an unruly force. Artists (primarily male ones) have struggled for centuries to keep the female body at bay by depicting it as harmonious and sealed. In this way, they have fabricated a sanitized version of female beauty as an object for consumption by a male viewer.

The power of the gaze is based on three main assumptions: 1) we can gain pleasure from looking at something; 2) a representation with erotic content can stir us without us performing any actions apart from looking; 3) the object of our gaze can be over-valued or devalued.

Here are a few fundamental concepts which can help us understand how the gaze works:

Scopophilia (from the Greek **scopein,** 'to look' + **philia**, 'love'): pleasure that comes from looking.

Voyeurism (from the French **voyeur,** 'one who sees'): excitement produced by viewing other bodies, unclothed or engaged in sexual intercourse.

Fetishism (from the Latin **facere**, 'to make' or **facticius**, 'artificial'): attraction to objects or bodily attributes associated with a sexual partner rather than with with her/his actual body.

Sadism (from the writings of the Marquis de Sade, 1740-1814): pleasure that comes from observing someone else's pain, whether or not we have inflicted it ourselves.

In scopophilia, the object of the gaze simply elicits pleasure; in voyeurism, it elicits pleasure to the extent that it can be seen as a sexual body; in fetishism, it is an idealized token of eroticism

The scopophiliac, the voyeur, the fetishist and the sadist derive pleasure from something other than the body itself. This 'something' may be the body as an object on display, as a work of art, as a commodity, as bleeding flesh. Or it may be a titillating symbol of sexuality: a shoe, a phallic car bonnet, a nightgown, a tattoo, a dog collar, etc. There are no known limits to the range of pleasures people may devise and enjoy. And pleasures based on looking/being looked at undoubtedly play important roles in all sorts of sexualities.

But when we reduce looking to the single controlling function of the gaze, we risk losing some of the body's most promising sources of pleasure. The gaze becomes a substitute for physical contact. And there's always a danger that in experiencing the other's body from a distance, we may lose touch with our own body as well.

the Body in the cyberculture

Outline

Cyberculture has redefined the body by interfacing it with various machines and computer-generated images. Many contemporary films and works of fiction are based on the 'cyberbody': a part-body which comments both on the myth of the perfect body and on the dread of human incompleteness.

cybernetics

Cyberculture highlights the merging of natural and technological forms. It proposes new forms of embodiment, new ways of exchanging signals in time and space and alternative forms of knowledge.

The word **cybernetics** was introduced in 1948 by the mathematician Norbert Wiener (1894-1964) in a book titled **Cybernetics, or Control and Communication in the Animal and the Machine**. Cybernetics derives from the Greek word 'kibernetes', which means 'steersman', to imply that control should be a form of 'steersmanship', not of 'dictatorship'.

Wiener believed that both biological bodies and mechanical bodies are **self-regulating systems.** Human bodies and machines are interrelated: both work in terms of control and communication. Communication is a **flow of information.**

Wiener divided the history of automata into four stages:

1. the Golemic age
(according to Jewish legends, the 'Golem' is a man made of clay and animated by the power of magical words; the Golem could be seen as a mythical predecessor of Frankenstein's monster)

2. the age of clocks
(17th and 18th centuries)

3. the age of steam
(late 18th and 19th centuries)

4. the age of communication and control
(the era of cybernetics)

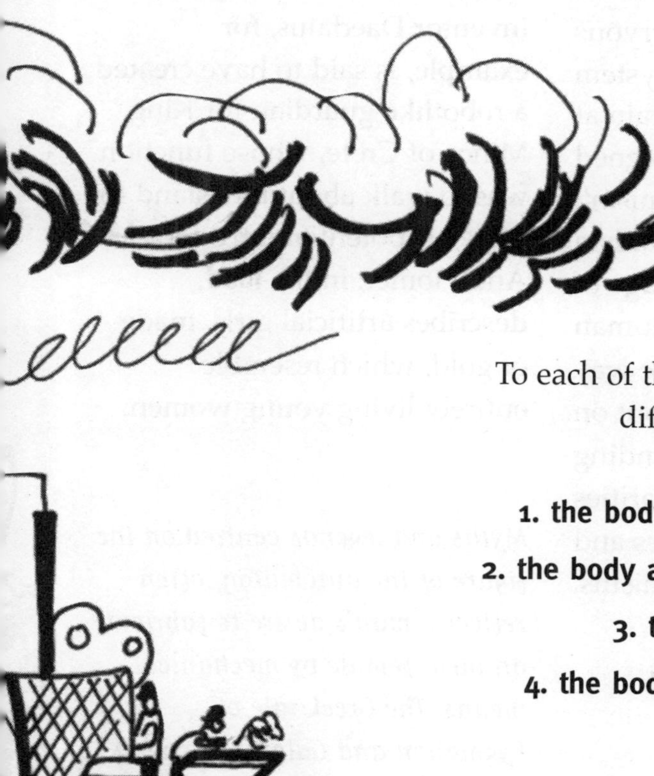

To each of these stages corresponds a different model of the body:

1. the body as a magical clay shape
2. the body as a clockwork mechanism
3. the body as a heat engine
4. the body as an electronic system

The body as an **electronic system** is a communications network, comparable to a machine. It takes in information through the senses and then acts on the information received. If the human body can be thought of as a machine, it is also possible to design machines which replicate the human organism. Such machines are based on the model of the nervous apparatus, a graded system of control with the brain at the top. A machine so designed is a 'cybernetic organism'. The cybernetic organism produced by the age of electronics mirrors the human body: not in the simplistic way of conventional robots but on the basis of an understanding of the structural similarities between machines and living organisms.

However, the idea of the **automaton** is a lot older than we may imagine. As a mechanical contraption able to imitate living things, the automaton is already present in the myths of ancient Greece. The mythical inventor Daedalus, for example, is said to have created a robotlike guardian for King Minos of Crete, whose function was to walk about the island to scare off potential intruders. And Homer, in the **Iliad,** describes artificial girls, made of gold, which resemble entirely living young women.

Myths and legends centred on the figure of the automaton, often reflect a man's desire to fabricate an ideal female by mechanical means. The Greek tale of Pygmalion and Galatea is one of the earliest examples of this trend. Films such as Hughes's ***Weird Science*** *and DeJarnatt's* ***Cherry 2000*** *are present day variations on a similar theme.*

The seventeenth century French philosopher **René Descartes** is said to have had a female automaton named Francine as a travelling companion. This rumour presents an intriguing paradox. Descartes championed the philosophy of rationalism **(see The Body and Philosophy).** Rationalism argues that the mind is superior to the body. It also states that humans are superior to machines because they **naturally** possess minds which machines can only **artificially** imitate. Why should Descartes pick a machine as a partner? Surely a real human being would have been more of an intellectual challenge! Yet Descartes would probably have regarded a meat-and-bones woman as an irrational creature whose body was likely to hamper the mind's well-being. Francine was possibly **thick** - as a machine - by the standards of the male brain, but still preferable to a 'capricious' female in the flesh. Francine's technobody would at least have offered an entity devoid of affects where the emotions were controlled by artificial reason.

Today, we don't always think of automata as humanoid in appearance: a robotic 'arm' equipped with surgical tools designed to assist a surgeon in performing a delicate operation doesn't look anything like a human arm, let alone a whole human body.

The Scottish anatomist and surgeon **Charles Bell (1774-1842)** was the first to compare biological organisms and human-made structures and machines. For example, he compared the body's bone structure to elements of architecture, and the heart and vascular system to pumps and pipes used in engineering.

The design of modern automata is the main concern of two related sciences:

1. ***Bio-engineering*** *focuses on the application of technological principles to the body. It studies the body's structure in terms of engineering, for example by looking at the mechanical qualities of different bodily substances, such as bone and muscle.*

2. ***Bionics*** *(from biological electronics) focuses on the application of biological processes to technology. It believes that certain 'design principles' present in the human body can be used in order to create new mechanical devices. The human body is a model for producing machines.*

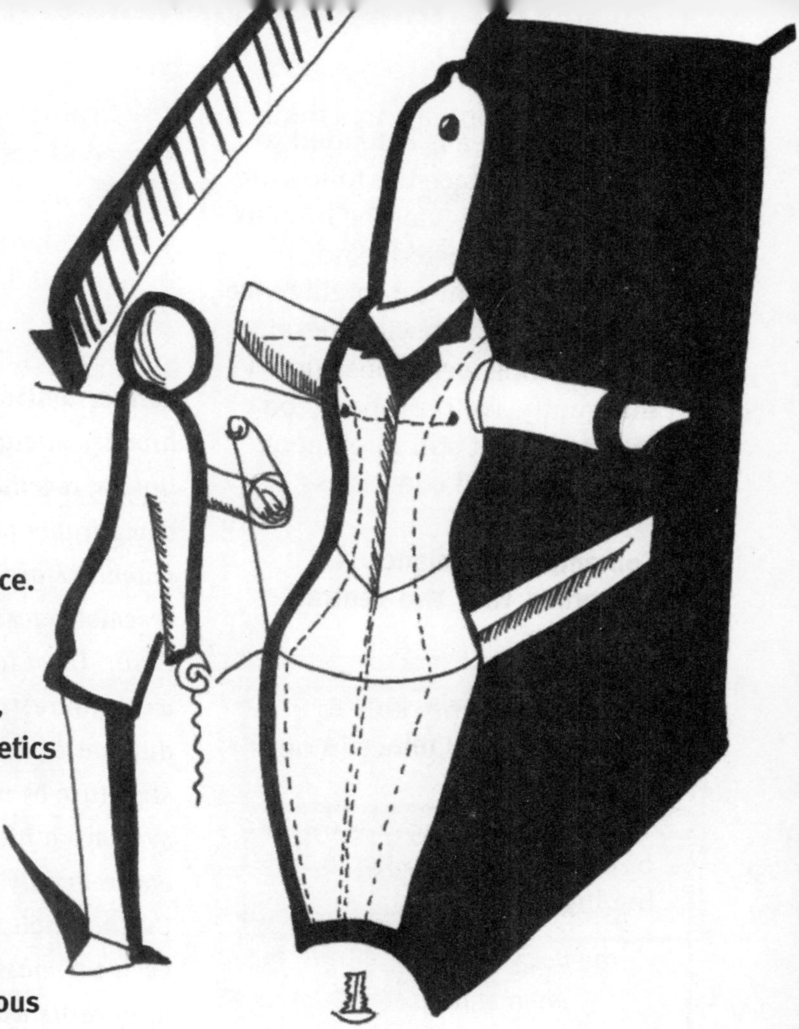

Bionics is also concerned with the question of whether machines are capable of intelligence. It is closely related to the field of *Artificial Intelligence*, the strand of cybernetics which explores whether machines simply 'appear' to be intelligent or are capable of developing autonomous mental processes.

The starting point of computer based artificial intelligence is the Turing machine, named after its designer, the British mathematician **Alan Mathison Turing (1912-54)**. This is what the machine consisted of: a long tape of squares, some with numbers on them, others blank. The machine read one square at a time and could move the tape backwards and forwards to read other squares.

This was the dawn of modern digital computers. In Turing's system, the machine's physical construction (its body) is irrelevant. It can be mechanical, electrical, or anything else. All that matters is that it can carry out certain instructions in order to solve specific problems.

When this idea is extended to the body, we face the following possibility: the way the human brain is constructed is not really important for intelligence or feelings or consciousness. If our brains were constructed differently, we'd probably be different - but still intelligent, perceiving and conscious.

Contemporary science is concerned with two central questions:

is a machine only able to 'simulate' intelligence in one limited area?

or could it possess general intelligence?

Connectionism *aims at producing broadly intelligent machines by linking together mechanical units comparable to neurons: such machines are supposed to resemble closely the human brain. For a long time, scientists were interested in devising automata which imitated the structure of the human nervous system - a hierarchical network controlled by a governing centre. On the whole, it turned out that even the most sophisticated apparatus was rather primitive in comparison with the human brain. Over the last couple of decades, science has been moving away from the idea of the automaton as a centralized system of control, and experimenting, instead, with* ***layering*** *(or 'subsumption architecture'). The automaton is assembled through the layering of separate units, each corresponding to a specific behaviour system, without any dominating ruler 'from above'.*

There are also scientists who are devoted to the creation of non-organic, yet lifelike, computer systems, e.g. systems based on 'neural networks' which imitate the workings of neurons in the human brain. This branch of research is known as Artificial Life, or **a-life:** it may lead to an alternative union of the biological and the electronic, the **biocomputer.**

cyberspace and cyberpunk

The term cyberspace **is generally used to describe a three-dimensional space in which the human body is surrounded at all times and on all sides by a flow of computer-based data and information, which the body can 'enter' and with which it can interact. Data and information are presented through multi-media techniques which can give people an illusion of movement and control.**

Cyberspace is closely connected with **Virtual Reality.** Virtual Reality, a phrase coined by **Jaron Lanier** in 1986, defines an environment in which reality is simulated through computers and in which the human body can experience artificially generated data as if they were coming from the natural world. People immersed in a virtual environment can actually experience the realistic feeling of inhabiting that world.

The user of Virtual Reality receives images and impressions from various mechanical devices attached to the user's body, to provide the impressions of sight, sound and touch. Stereo headphones supply sounds; head-mounted goggles, or **eyephones,** supply computer-generated images; wired gloves, or **datagloves,** and computerized suits, or **datasuits**, supply the sense of touch. These devices are also able to monitor the body's movements, so that what the user sees or feels changes according to her/his movements.

A person could move through a computer-generated house which s/he might wish to live in even before the house is built; or visit simulated holiday resorts before actually booking the holiday. These experiences are not the same as watching a film, because the person can interact with his/her environment in ways which cinema and video cannot offer. In addition, different people may experience these spaces at the same time without physically occupying the same location: the same information can be communicated across a broad network via modems.

A variation on this theme is offered by Bigelow's **Strange Days.** In this film, any event (actual, imagined, wished for, feared) can be translated into portable software. People can then re-live it with the aid of a wired contraption placed on the head like a cap. What they re-experience, however, is not simply the superficial appearance of facts that have already taken place, but also feelings, thoughts and emotions which accompanied the occurrence. They can thus enter other people's brains and their future projections.

*In Virtual Reality, we encounter two forms of **life**: The life of the natural body 'inside' the mechanical devices and the life of the computer networks which produce visual and other effects. The body's life is inseparable from that of the computer networks that interact with it.*

Technology has become a living species: a 'body' in its own right. In Virtual Reality, machines come to life and acquire organicity.

But there are other everyday situations in which important similarities are set up between human bodies and machines, as though to remind us that they are interchangeable.

Many computer scientists and cognitive psychologists are keen on describing the human mind as a computer, and vice versa. Others tend to **anthropomorphize** the computer:

Computers have a 'memory', 'cells' and 'tissues' in the form of electronic networks; 'blood' in the form of electricity; 'illnesses' in the form of viruses; and 'medical treatment' in the form of disinfectants. There are even quite explicit hints at similarities between computers' infections and HIV/AIDS, based on the idea that computers become contaminated due to 'promiscuous' behaviour on the part of their users (for example, the insertion of alien disks into their machines). Computers 'are born', 'die' and even 'get married' (that is, linked up to a networked system). Adverts for computers often exploit this 'humanizing' imagery.

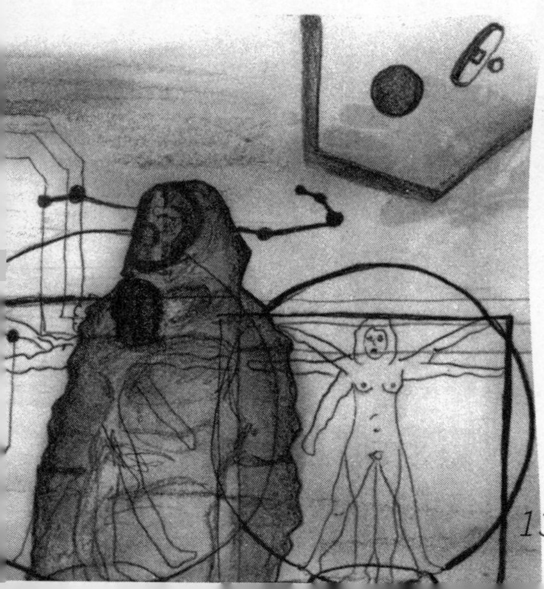

*In some fictional texts, computers are invested with powerful feelings and desires: in Kubrick's **2001: A Space Odyssey,** for instance, the spaceship's computer HAL is more emotional than the astronauts themselves. In Cammell's **Demon Seed**, Susan, a psychiatrist, is raped by artificial intelligence.*

The association of computer technology with human physicality and sexuality can be read in two ways. Some think that the fusion of body and machine signals the 'disappearance' of the body from contemporary culture. The body, they claim, is eaten up by technology, reduced to dead meat. Others believe that this fusion promises alternative forms of erotic fulfilment: it serves to extend our understanding of what a body is, can be, or might be and opens up opportunities for experiment and recombination.

The term **cyberpunk,** first used by the writer **Bruce Bethke** in 1983, is now generally used to describe a fictional genre centred on the works of **William Gibson** and other writers. Cyberpunk is sci-fi but its points of reference are cybernetics and biotechnology rather than spaceships and robots. Science does not inhabit an inaccessible fortress but is actually everywhere. The **punk** element in the word cyberpunk hints at a defiant attitude based in urban street culture. Cyberpunk's characters are people on the fringe of society: outsiders, losers and loonies, struggling for survival on a planet filled with junk.

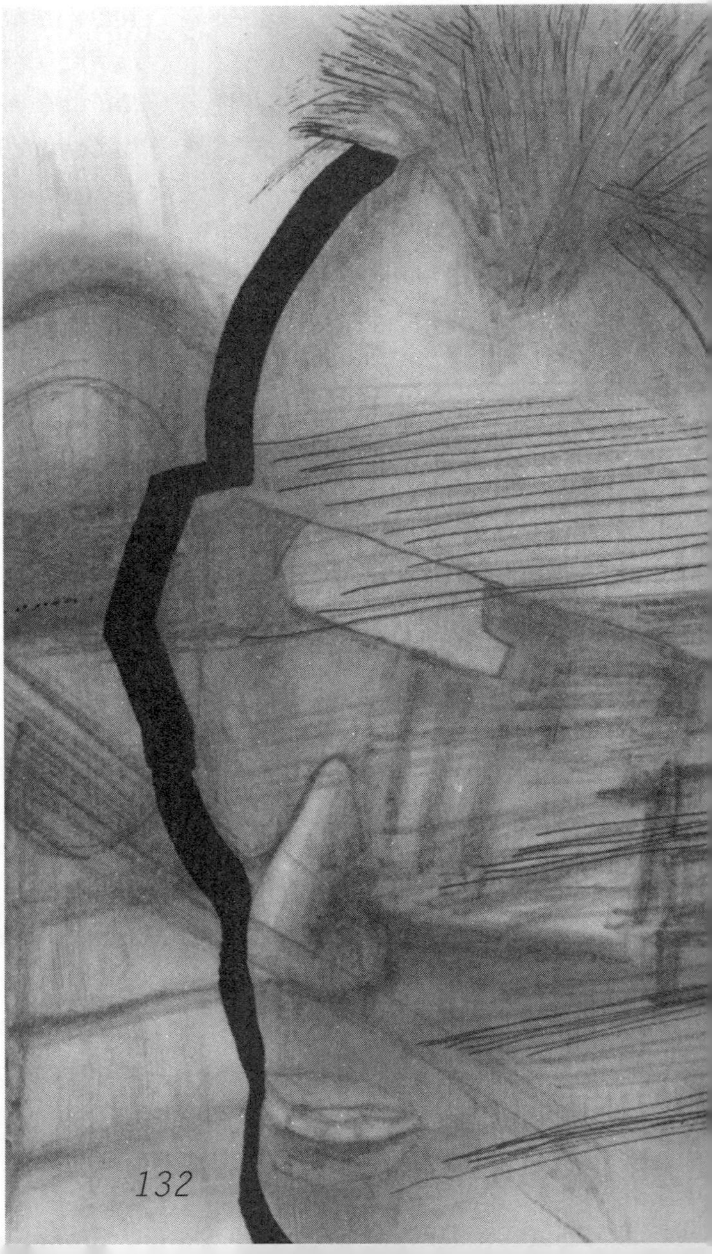

Cyberpunk presents visions of the future based on the extensive application of the idea of cyberspace and its impact on the body. The terms 'cyberspace' and 'virtual reality' first appeared in William Gibson's novel **Neuromancer** (1984). This is the story of 'computer cowboy' Case (a computer cowboy is an illicit operator in the Net), of the 'Matrix' (a global representation of the databanks of all the computers in the human system) and of the deceptions, crimes and power struggles associated with its users.

Biotech plays a big part in **Neuromancer.** Flesh can be 'vat-grown' and any organ can be lifted out of the body and replaced with a brand new one. A huge black market network trades incessantly body parts and genetic materials. Surgery can enhance the body's powers in countless ways. Molly, one of the main characters, has mirror-shade implants over her eyes which allow her to see in the dark, as well as lethal retractable blades inserted under each of her fingernails.

There are conflicting interpretations of the messages put forward by cyberpunk. Some see it as the apocalyptic vision of a culture where people are subjected to ruthless communication networks and totally disconnected from one another. This culture has little or no respect for the living body. Gibson's console cowboys actually leave their bodies behind when they jack into cyberspace. Similarly, Topo, the protagonist of the cartoon book **Cyberpunk**, longs to 'leave the meat behind' and become pure consciousness in the virtual spaces of the 'Playing Field'.

Others see cyberpunk in more positive terms, as the vision of a future world where technology enhances humanity by opening up fresh forms of creativity and interraction. The body itself can be rethought in imaginative terms. Accepting our fusion with machines of all sorts may help us think about both our bodies and our identities differently and more flexibly.

In some cyberpunk texts, people actually change their identities as easily as we would change our clothes. In G.A. Effinger's trilogy **When Gravity Fails, A Fire in the Sun,** and **The Exile Kiss,** for example, all the characters need to do, in order to acquire alternative identities, is to chip software directly into their wired brains. The software consists of personality patterns ('moddies') which can be purchased from 'modshops'. In W.J. Williams' novel **Hardwired,** characters are able to alter their sexual identities just as easily.

Gibson explores similar ideas in the short story ***Johnny Mnemonic.*** *Thousands of data are stashed in the protagonist's head as so many megabytes. His brain has been remodelled through microsurgery to resemble a computer. He cannot know or remember any of the information stored in his head, until he meets a cyborg dolphin trained as a 'superconducting quantum interference detector' (Squid) who can detect the passwords buried in the chips in Johnny's head. This gives him access to everything people have put inside him to huge financial advantage.* ***Johnny Mnemonic*** *is also a story about memory. It asks: who owns whose memories? It exemplifies the fact that we never live simply with our own memories: the media, for example, implant prosthetic memories into our brains all the time.*

But how likely are we to become computers?

Can the computer mentality embrace everything human?

Computers can no doubt achieve astonishing results in the simulation of real space. But they still leave certain questions unanswered. This idea is explored in a short story by Italo Calvino entitled 'The Burning of the Abominable House', which he wrote in response to the question, raised by IBM in 1973: could a story be written using a computer? Calvino's protagonist, a computer expert, sets out to write his murder story by trying to establish the number of different ways in which his computer could process and combine a given set of data: characters, their personalities, their possible reasons for committing the crime, the weapons which could have been used, etc. Technology helps the writer work out a large number of possible combinations and permutations. But it cannot reduce the creative act to a purely mathematical exercise. The writer, in spite of himself, cannot help identifying with the characters and imagining their faces, bodies and gestures. The human mind is not an anonymous machine because there are ethical, bodily and emotional concerns which the machine cannot address and which the mind cannot avoid addressing.

The computer is a creative tool: maybe in the future all fictional worlds will become databases, as the character of the fiction writer in Gore Vidal's **Duluth** hopes. But this doesn't mean that the computer is any more imaginative than the typewriter ever was. This doesn't make the mind 'better' than the machine in any real way. It simply shows that humans and machines, though largely interchangeable, cannot wholly **become** each other. Cyberculture does not aim at turning humans into machines or machines into humans. Rather, it highlights their inevitable interrelation.

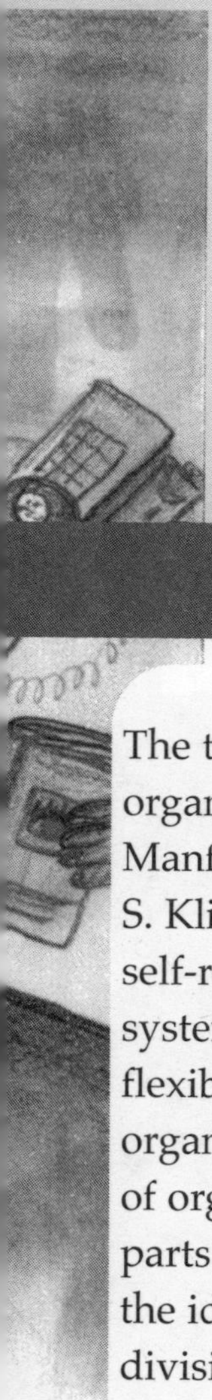

cyborgs

The term **cyborg** (cybernetic organism) was put forward by Manfred E. Clynes and Nathan S. Kline in 1960 to describe a self-regulating man-machine system, supposed to be more flexible than the human organism thanks to the fusion of organic and mechanical parts. The cyborg embodies the idea that there are no clear divisions between the non-human and the human, the technological and the biological, the artificial and the natural.

There are two main issues at stake in the cyborg body:

1. the cyborg is not simply a fantastic creature: many people's bodies are cyborg-like to various degrees;

2. the cyborg embodies two opposite fantasies: that of the sealed body and that of the unbounded body.

The first point can be explained by looking at the technological/medical reshaping of the body. Prostheses (i.e. devices which replace a missing part of the body) and artificial organs have been around for a long time and exhibit now increasing levels of sophistication. At present, virtually every body part can be replaced. The brain and nervous system are still exceptions, but for how long?

*Scientist **Hans Moravec** believes that in the not too distant future, it will be possible to transfer mental functions to computer software. This process, which Moravec calls **transmigration,** may take some time to materialize in practice, but it has already found expression in the world of fiction. In Rudy Rucker's novel **Software,** for example, an elderly scientist agrees to have his brain functions taken out of his body by powerful automata, in exchange for an immortal robot body of his own. He then finds out, much to his disappointment, that immortality doesn't give him absolute power: his mental patterns have been appropriated and stored in a Mr Frostee ice-cream truck.*

Cosmetic surgery, biotechnology, genetic engineering, and the replacement of organic functions by biochip implants show that there is simply no such thing as a pure body.

Let's now consider the second point. On one level, the cyborg presents a pure, clean, hard, tight and uncontaminated body. It offers the ideal of a body which does not eat, drink, cry, sweat, urinate, defecate, menstruate, ejaculate: a body which does not suffer any illnesses and does not die. This 'Puritanical' body without secretions and indiscretions stands for the dream of a whole antiseptic world freed of infection and pollution. The fantasy of a pure self, disengaged from nature, perpetuates traditional western views about the body's worthlessness by comparison with the mind.

There is a fantasy of omnipotence: the mechanical parts which replace ordinary anatomical parts are supposed to enhance the body's power potential. There is a fantasy of order and purity: the image of the cyborg as the unsoiled body, cleansed of the organism's messy reality. And there is also a fantasy of completion: if the natural body is lacking and fragmented, the machine may make it whole. The cyborg is both a means of making the body cleaner and stronger and a way of acknowledging that the body needs artificial props if it is to survive at all.

Verhoeven's **Robocop** and Cameron's **The Terminator** and its sequel **Terminator 2: Judgment Day** are popular dramatizations of the cyborg theme. The cyborg body presented by these films is strong, hardly susceptible to injury and pain and able to self-repair very quickly. It is also a very **masculine** body: in western culture, it is the male shape that is seen as 'sealed' and bounded, and the female one, by contrast, that is seen as 'leaky' and unbounded.

But the muscular and virile cyborg body is also, inevitably, a hybrid of organic and mechanical parts - and therefore an impure being. It can only display its strength by putting on an 'armour'. In both ***Terminator*** *films, the Terminator makes his first appearance on this planet as a vulnerable and naked figure, folded up in a foetal position. He gains his phallic power and stereotypically masculine aggressiveness through the violent acquisition of leather gear and weapons.*

The cyborg combines vulnerability and strength. Technology is capable of policing the natural body's uncertain boundaries. But it also unsettles further the body's boundaries through the intersection of the human and the non-human.

Interestingly, cyberculture also offers a male type - the 'computer hacker' or 'computer nerd' - who, though biologically male, is weak, overweight, unattractive and addicted to technology as if it were a drug: the nerd's faulty body is definitely at odds with the cyborg's invincible body. Gibson's computer cowboys similarly depart from the muscular Schwarzenegger model. Their 'penetration' of the Matrix (which, incidentally, means womb) gives them an active male role. But on the whole, they are actually quite passive and physically inactive, since their activities consist fundamentally of cerebral operations.

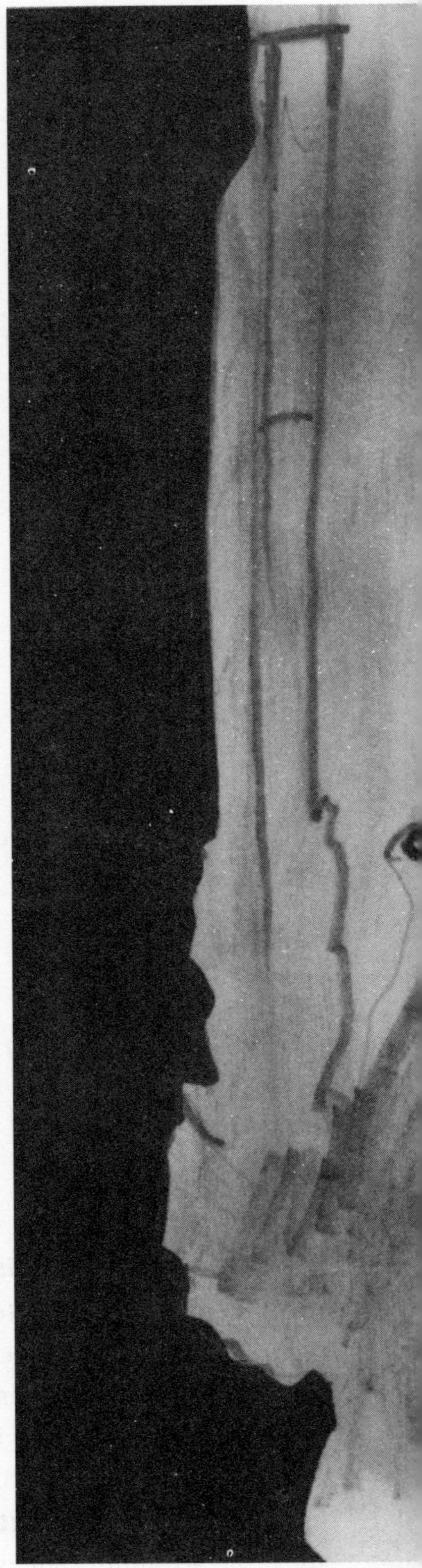

The cyborg's own sexual role is not without contradictions: although mainstream films present the cyborg as a hypermasculine figure, endowed with tremendous physical strength and a propensity to kill and destroy, they also make room for more benevolent dispositions. The Terminator in **Terminator 2,** in particular, operates as a kind of surrogate father. Nor are the female characters presented in cyborg films uniformly passive. In **The Terminator**, Sarah Connor destroys the Terminator, and in the sequel, she features as a muscular and ruthless fighter. Her fate is associated essentially with motherhood, but she hardly fits into the nurturing woman stereotype. Some feminist writers see the model of the 'muscular angry woman' as an embodiment of patriarchal values, and as a fetish produced by male fears, especially the fear of the unbounded female body.

Others see it as an ideal to be aspired to by women who are still subjected to injustice. Yet a character like Sarah cannot be viewed unproblematically as either a male fetish or a feminist vision: she incorporates conflicting possibilities and, to this extent, reinforces the sense of ambiguity typical of cyborg narratives generally.

The paradox surrounding the figure of the cyborg could be compared to the ambivalent situation experienced by a person wearing a prosthesis (artificial limbs, harnesses, metal rods, spectacles, wonder bras and bums, shoulder pads, high heels, silicon injections, penile implants...).
The prosthesis makes us 'more able' - we can now see better, walk better, fuck better - and therefore gives us a more ideal conception of our bodies. But it also reminds us of our failings, our need for support, the loss of the 'whole' body that didn't need the prosthesis in the first place. The prosthesis gives us a double identity: the **better** self and the **failing** self. It refines our capacities and reminds us of our incapacities.
It strengthens the edges of our bodies and at the same time blurs them by compounding us with inorganic 'bits'.
J.G.Ballard's novel **Crash** (1973) explores fairly extreme possibilities of fusion between the physical self and the mechanical non-self:

conventions about sexuality, as a celebration of the body's creativity. However, its focus is undeniably on the idea that the human and the non-human, life and death, pleasure and pain, creation and destruction can become indistinguishable.

the merging of bodies and cars, of bodies through cars and car-inflicted wounds, of bodies and prostheses made necessary by ghastly car injuries, all amount to monumental sexual climaxes. The body's boundaries are expanded at the same time as they are violated. The novel lends itself to contrasting interpretations, as a cautionary tale about the triumph of an inhuman technology, as a rejection of all moral and psychological

The union of biology and technology produces both bliss and horror, enjoyment and revulsion. Do people experience pleasure in the presence of their prostheses or do they resent them? Does the idea of being so closely associated with an artificial body 'disgust' us? Are we worried about the extent to which our body could be 'violated' by artificial props?

In **Robocop,** the body is literally rebuilt through technology. The dominant concern is the violation of humanity by the machine. To this extent, the film is a fable about the struggle between good and evil, where the 'goody' is the human mind as the last remainder of the original human self, and the 'baddy' is the technological body imposed on that mind. That Murphy is 'more human' than a machine (although it is by no means clear how much of his body has been salvaged beside his brain) is made clear by the fact that he goes on being haunted by human concerns even after he has been engulfed in a computerized existence. He is still able to experience deep emotional pain, particularly when he remembers his past life as a husband and father. He is also physically superior to the clumsy android Ed 209. OCP (Omni Consumer Products) believe that Murphy's personal identity can be erased through reprogramming. But Murphy retains the desire to break free because, somewhat magically, he has retained his will. The mechanical being 'Robocop' remains human, in the logic of the series, as long as Murphy retains a mind as the 'essence' of humaneness.

The situation is somewhat more complicated in an android-based film like **Blade Runner,** where it is difficult to draw clear distinctions between the mind and the body, the human mind and the non-human body: the replicants are artificial constructions, but are also able to pass as human beings and to display human emotions because human memories have been installed in their systems. Here, memories do not say anything about the past as lived experience - the past was never lived - but rather construct the present. They fashion cyberpeople **as if** they had a past.

To recap: 1) many 'ordinary bodies' have features of the cyborg body; 2) the cyborg body is both whole and hybrid; 3) cyborg fictions remind us that our own bodies are culturally framed yet lacking. *Let's take a closer look at Cameron's Terminators as illustrations of these ideas.*

To begin with, the Terminators are presented explicitly as *non-human.*

1. Their vision is computerized and this distinguishes them instantly from 'natural' human beings; they do not see the world in the way humans do, and we - the human spectators - can witness that this is the case. The cyborg is unmasked: it resembles the human body, but the resemblance is only an illusion. There is nothing truly human underneath the surface.

2. They do not experience pain - they 'sense injuries'; even when they claim to understand what human suffering is, they only do so in terms of mechanical programmes.

Yet, the cyborg is human in so far as it symbolizes human fears and anxieties. First of all, the figure of the cyborg reminds us that if machines can assume the semblance of humanity, humanity could, in turn, be interfaced with machines. Secondly, the cyborg is a projection of human fears about the future, about the possibility of the whole planet becoming a battlefield peopled by mindless machines thrashing one another in the blind pursuit of absolute power. In both cases, the cyborg is construed as something 'at odds' with humanity. But there is another side to the game: the cyborg does not simply embody human preoccupations, it also gives human beings a means of understanding themselves.

*The **Terminator** films suggest that human beings need cyborgs in order to assert their humanity - to go on believing that they are 'still' human, after all. Take **Terminator 2**, in particular. Here, we are faced with two different cyborg bodies: the 'old' Cyberdine Systems Model 101, capable of many miraculous things but still, in some ways, stuck with its body, and the 'new' T-1000, made exclusively of liquid metal and therefore able to reinvent its body endlessly. The 'old' model is turned into a hero of sorts, while the 'new' model is made into the bad guy. The new model is just too inhuman: its body 'happens' to look human at times, but is equally convincing as an inanimate object. T-1000 cannot be seen as a friend because nothing about its structure and acts commit it finally to the human camp. 101, on the other hand, retains enough of a connection with 'real' human bodies to count as a friend, to 'seem' human even though it obviously isn't.*

More than this, 101 is able to remind real humans of what being human means or could mean. John and Sarah need 101 to remind them of their own humanity: of what it means to cry, to love, to lose a friend, to feel pain. Of course, all this may sound like a bit of a dream: the friendly, semi-human cyborg is, like any other cyborg, a fruit of the human imagination. Turning a cyborg into a Walt Disney kind of amiable pet doesn't mean, automatically, that all associations between the human body and the mechanical body will be fun.

However, if we move from the world of 'dreams' to that of social 'reality', we find that many of the concerns explored through fictions of the kind we have just looked at are also at the forefront of serious philosophical and theoretical investigation. The cyborg is no less a creature of cultural reality than it is a creature of fantasy: doubts and uncertainties about the association of human and mechanical bodies presented in popular movies and novels mirror similar doubts and uncertainties about the meaning and consequences of living in a computer-saturated environment. Whether we think this is a 'good' or a 'bad' thing, it is undeniable that electronic media have transformed and are transforming profoundly the very meaning of cultural identity.

The 'Internet' plays a big part in all this. As a global collection of computer systems (including electronic mail, database and general communication systems), the Net has become enormously popular in recent years.

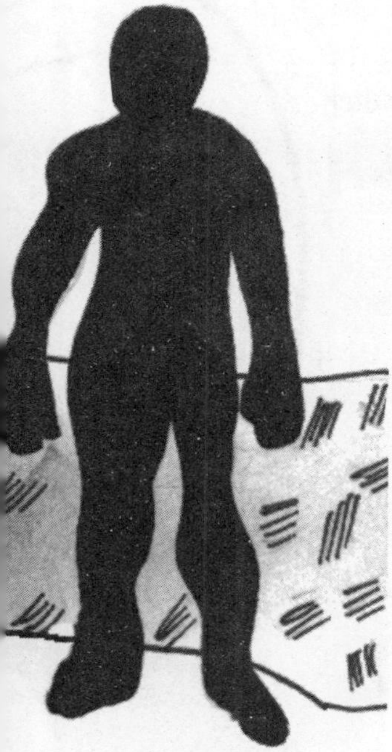

Surveys carried out in the mid-1990s indicate that there are about 30 million users around the planet (and 4 million computers, and 50,000 plus networks involved in the operation). There are also places for 'meeting' on the Internet, for example bulletin boards such as the 'Well', electronic mail services and cybercafes. And this is by no means the end of the tale: there is every sign that by 2005, the entire world could, in principle, be connected. Moreover, 'information superhighways' (mechanisms for transmitting information extra-rapidly from and to any point in the network) will produce a massive flow of information.

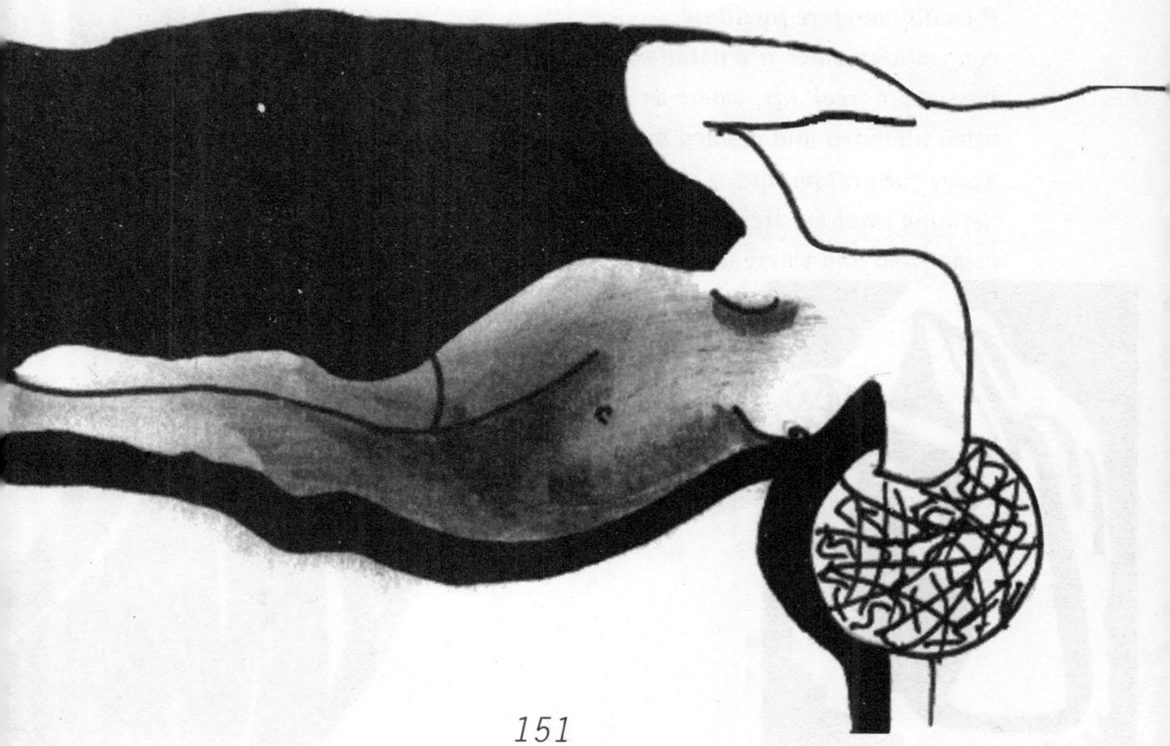

Many believe that inhabiting this kind of world is liberating. They maintain that such an environment opens new opportunities for the exchange of ideas and images. Mass computerization becomes a 'democratic machine' which is able to stimulate creativity, mobility, access and communication. Knowledge is no longer dominated by governments and bureaucracy. It belongs to anybody and everybody. We can all take part in a new 'community'. This global community would not be tied to traditional concepts of 'territory', 'nation', 'state' or 'tradition'. What's more, the Net enables us to interact with total strangers without any obvious clues about their age, race, gender, sexual proclivities, social status, occupation, etc. It could therefore facilitate connections which are not always possible in 'real' life, where we are often inhibited and divided by a heavy cultural bundle of signs defining what we are, where we come from and where we belong.

But there are also many critics of computerized culture who believe that technology fragments us and distances us from one another.

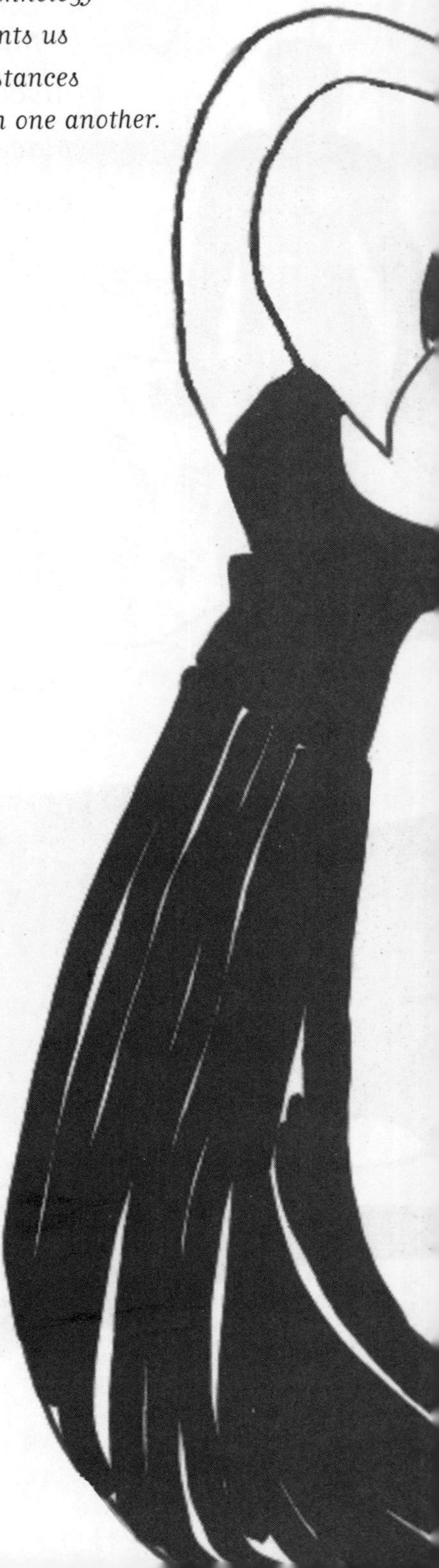

The positive approach to mass computerization suggests that our bodies may interact with one another in more creative and less prejudiced ways. The negative approach suggests that our bodies will only become spare parts, since computer networks deny any physical connection, and have no time for those who are still hungry.

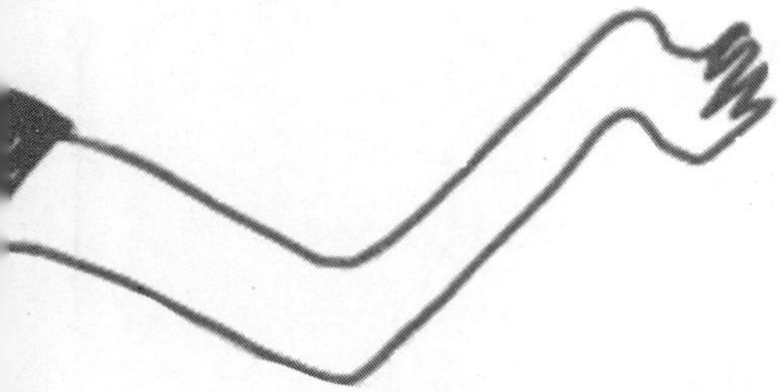

Both positions come together in the cyborg body as an understanding of the fact that human bodies and identities are always partial and contradictory.

All the operations we perform to acquire knowledge through computer networks, they argue, are solitary activities. Moreover, not everybody on the planet, as things stand, has equal access to computer-generated information: does this amount to a 'techno-apartheid'? If so, does technology really care about those who are left out or left behind? Is there really a community global enough to accommodate everybody's needs?

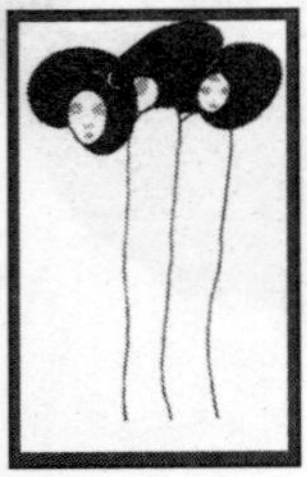

Conclusion: Incorporations

the corpus

The Latin word for 'body', corpus, has survived in modern English in two main forms: **corpus** and **incorporation**. Both illuminate contemporary ways of thinking about the body. We still use the word **corpus** today to describe **the body of works** produced by a writer, or an artist, and sometimes to refer to a cluster of legends, stories or myths. This usage of the word **corpus** indicates that we like to think about the body as something whole, as an all-encompassing category that allows us to group disparate things together.

The word corpus also appears in the term incorporation. By this, people normally mean either of two things:

1. We 'incorporate' people, objects and ideas when we integrate them or absorb them into a system. We are constantly trying to incorporate other people, racially and sexually for example. And we also strive to incorporate our environments: plants, animals and other life forces. We do this by means of political systems, economic organizations and technology. In this case, as in that of the literary corpus as an organizing structure, incorporation is fundamentally a process of unification.

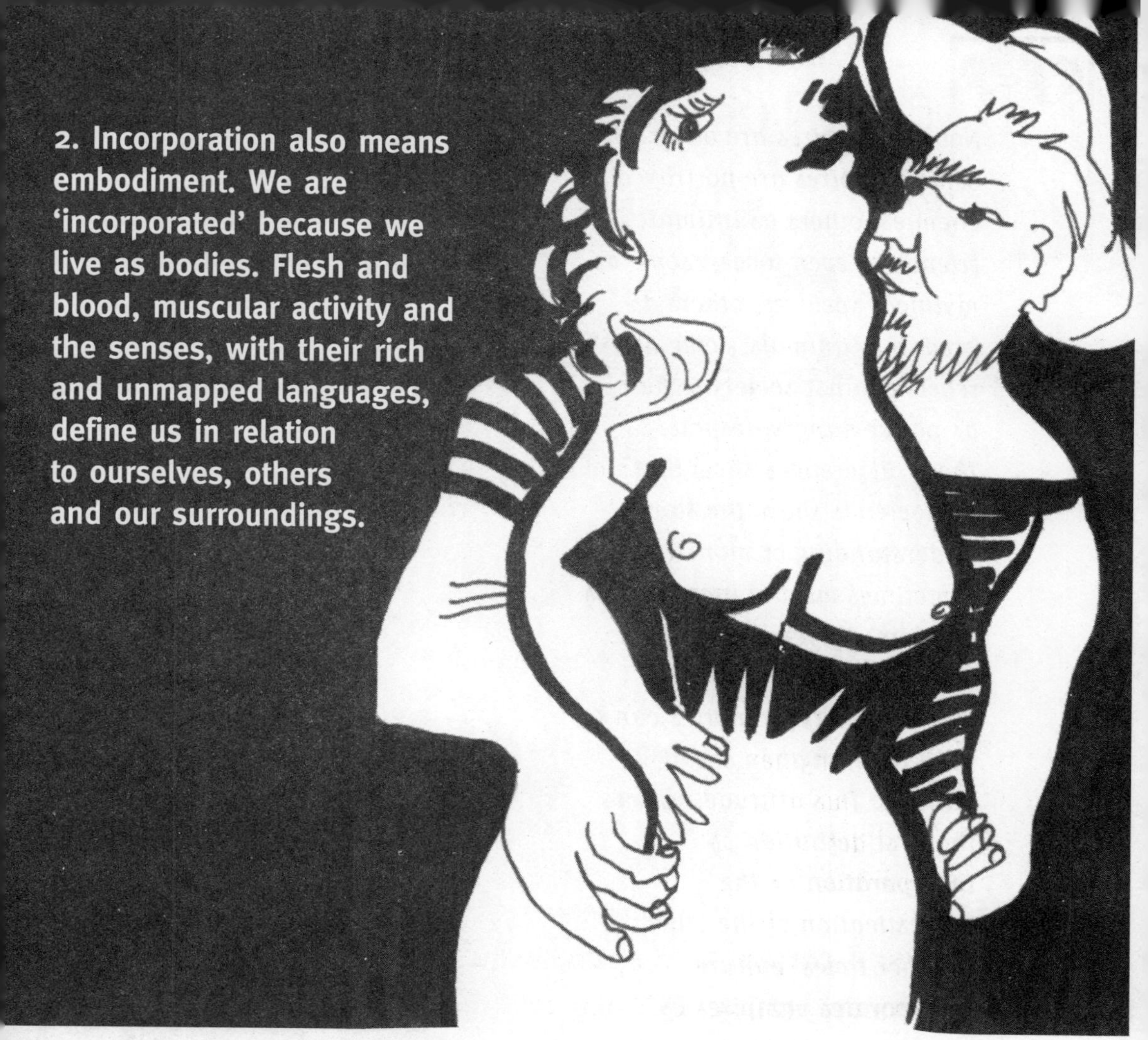

The second definition of incorporation challenges the ideal of unity. It reminds us that we experience the world in a fragmentary fashion, through multiple channels, physical urges, pleasures and pains. The scraps of information we glean can seldom be tied up in a neat bundle.

In the first part of this book, the **vampire** was cited as a particularly intriguing type of hybrid body. In this final section, I return to the theme of vampirism to give some illustrations of how incorporation works.

the vampire's body

Not all vampires are alike. Some vampires are portrayed as enemies, others as intimate friends or even lovers; some as mythical spectres, others as predatory animals; some as rebels against society, others as power-hungry despots. These differences show that not all societies share the same understanding of monstrosity. Sometimes culture ***incorporates*** *vampires by repressing them and segregating them from mortal society: vampires can be used to strengthen social barriers. This attitude reflects the first definition of* ***incorporation*** *as the domestication of the other. At other times, culture* ***incorporates*** *vampires by accepting that the vampire's body is not a monstrous aberration but rather the embodiment of widespread fantasies and yearnings. This attitude mirrors the second definition of* ***incorporation.*** *It stresses that there isn't a single legitimate body because our feelings and ideas can take many disparate shapes.*

Before Stoker's **Dracula** (1897), vampires are often depicted as close friends. Both Lord

Ruthven in Polidori's **The Vampyre** (1819) and Sir Francis Varney in Rymer's **Varney the Vampire** (1845-47) treasure their homoerotic friendships with humans. In J.Sheridan Le Fanu's **Carmilla** (1872) friendship develops into lesbian love: Carmilla and Laura share everything, even dreams. These vampires offer total intimacy: humans and vampires **incorporate** each other.

*But in **Dracula,** things are quite different. The vampire is solitary. He gives humans a pretext for teaming together under a common purpose: the destruction of the monster. But Dracula himself doesn't enjoy any companionship. A foreign hybrid, he is excluded from society and condemned to silence. With Stoker, the vampire becomes a hideous enemy, a beast. This is mainly because Stoker uses the vampire to give shape to the phobias of his society. The fear of the blood-drinker, of bodily infection and of irrational behaviour sum up cultural and political anxieties of the late nineteenth century: the dread of contamination of Britain and British blood by foreign countries; of venereal disease (believed to come from Eastern Europe); of female sexuality as predatory. All these fears have to do with the desire to protect the body's boundaries, both personal and collective.*

Dracula can be read in two ways.

One. It tells us that the other is utterly evil and must be exterminated. The other is the blood-drinker. But it is also the 'unruly' woman who indulges in sex for its own sake. The other must be **incorporated** (tamed, trapped) to restore the social fabric. In this reading, **Dracula** is a story of redemption. The annihilation of the vampire's body is a way of asserting British virtues against the alien intruder. And it is also a way of reminding us that the only acceptable parts for the female body to play are maternal and domestic. Here **incorporation** amounts to the celebration of **one proper body** - a body nourished by pure blood and chaste behaviour.

Two **Dracula** also shows that the other is not easily got rid of. The other is not something that lives **outside** the bodies and minds of so-called civilized people. It is **inside** all of us, often in the form of repressed sexual longings. **Dracula** is largely about the explosive release of suppressed Victorian libido. The novel oozes with eroticism. When the vampire 'bites', it penetrates the body in highly sexual ways. **The vampire is everywhere.** In this reading, **incorporation** amounts to the recognition that vampirism could be a part of any body. The body is not a unified object but a compound of clashing desires.

Vampires, then, *incorporate* or *embody* the values and anxieties of the cultures in which they are born. Consider another example, this time borrowed from cinema.

*One of the most famous filmic vampires is the actor **Bela Lugosi,** who acted in the 1931 version of **Dracula.** His performance says much about the America of the time. He is deliberately outlandish, eccentric, aristocratic and old-fashioned. In other words, he is everything a 'proper' American **shouldn't** be in the 1930s. The reason he is regarded as a monster is not that he is a* *blood-sucking beast. What makes him anomalous is the fact that the values he embodies are incompatible with those of the society he dwells in.*

As we turn to the late twentieth century, the picture changes again. In Anne Rice's **Vampire Chronicles**, vampires don't attach themselves to mortals. They are only interested in their fellow vampires. Maybe this is a comment on late twentieth-century tendencies to push all that is considered abnormal into a category of its own. This is a way of preventing any dialogue among different bodies which could result in 'contagion'. The AIDS epidemic, in particular, has prompted many people to think of **incorporation** as pollution. If for Dracula blood was life, in the context of AIDS blood brings to mind ghastly death.

***The Vampire Chronicles** also comment on the contemporary body in other ways. For one thing, they view the body as the victim of a crisis of authority. Rice's main vampires are beautiful and lethal but often don't know what to do with themselves. When their bodies have had enough, they enter states of total inertia or even seek death through self-destruction. Though inhuman, they're tied to their bodies all the time. They are as incorporated as anything human could ever be.*

The male body's power is also questioned. Louis and Lestat try to be 'fathers' but fail miserably. They make Claudia's body but cannot control its desires because they can't know what it's like to have an adult mind incorporated in a child's body.

Rice's characters have the means of tracing the vampire body back to ancient history but cannot incorporate their real sources. They find out that the first vampire, the Egyptian queen Akasha, was made into one by a spirit, Amel. But there's no final way of knowing who or what produced the spirit in the first place.

Knowledge of the past is supposed to enhance the vampires' powers. In fact, it crushes them. The vampire's body is the epitome of a body without origin. It frustrates all aspirations to discover where we come from. Looking back into the past is as futile as looking towards the future.

The authority of science is also undermined in ***The Chronicles.*** *In* ***Dracula****, science was the primary means of destroying the monster. Van Helsing's handling of Lucy's body was a superstitious ritual but it was also a scientific experiment. In Rice's books, science is associated with modern technology, and technology with gadgets which may be fun but don't really improve life in significant ways. In* ***Dracula*** *the body was* ***incorporated*** *by science as the supreme form of knowledge and power. In the* ***Chronicles****, the vampire body* ***incorporates*** *science, but science is just an array of fashionable toys.*

Vampirism is ultimately about the collapse of bodily barriers. Stoker's **Dracula** was obsessed with retaining all sorts of distinctions (between mortal and undead, male and female, British and non-British, etc.) because it was giving voice to the fear of the unknown. But what happens if this fear is taken away? Well, perhaps the vampire becomes a metaphor for a body that is neither sealed nor in awe of its boundaries but rather open, 'spongy', able to **incorporate** and be **incorporated** by several identities.

Dracula's animalism was seen as repulsive. But the vampire's shape-shifting body is also a positive assertion of ***all*** *bodies' protean identities.*

Vampires *incorporate* their natures into our own, by either entering or transforming them. This means that as they *incorporate* themselves into us, we i*ncorporate* ourselves into them.

a body-without-organs

When we think of the body as an **organism**, what we have in mind is a unitary structure in which all the parts relate to one another. Not only are the organs interrelated, they are also organized hierarchically, for not all organs are regarded as equally 'important' or 'powerful'. The idea of a unified organism pictures the body as a bounded **territory**. It is comparable to the notion of a nation-state protected by inviolable frontiers.

Gilles Deleuze and **Felix Guattari** question this view of the body. They believe that the body is not monolithic but fluid, sprawling, seeping and fragmented. After all, we don't experience our bodies as synthetic wholes. By and large we experience parts of our bodies.

Deleuze and Guattari argue that the bounded body is a myth produced by ideology. It reflects the capitalist urge to accumulate, to prevent property from spilling over the edge of its owner's domain. A watertight body that doesn't leak, exude or discharge is like a storehouse where riches can be kept without them ever seeing the light of day.

The type of body favoured by Deleuze and Guattari is a **body-without-organs**: a body that is not subjected to constraining definitions of its various parts, of each part's relation to the others, and of each part's function or meaning.

If the unified organism is a bounded 'territory', the body-without-organs is, by contrast, **deterritorialized**. It has no definitive form or meaning. It doesn't speak **a** language but **all** languages, it is not **a** machine but **all** machines.

Societies strive to give the body a stable shape but corporeality is wayward, flickering and restless. The body's **manyness** cannot be limited to the oneness of cultural identity. A lot of the time, we cannot even understand what we are seeing. We strain our eyes into the distance to see what is actually at hand. What we'd like to see dances in and out of the shadows cast by our own clouded vision.

This does not mean that having a body, or being a body, is a curse. What it means is that there is no unity, that life is a complex and fragile structure that cannot be reduced to an organic whole.

It also warns us against the desire to assimilate others: at the same time as we incorporate other life forms, we are also incorporated by them. We are born, grow and pass away by merging all the time with other nascent, growing or dying bodies.

corpography

Adler, K. and Pointon, M. (eds.), (1993), The Body Imaged: The Human Form and Visual Culture Since the Renaissance, Cambridge: Cambridge U.P.

Adorno, T. and Horkheimer, M. (1989), Dialectic of Enlightenment, trans. J.Cumming, London and New York: Verso.

Auerbach, N. (1995), Our Vampires, Ourselves, London and Chicago: Chicago U.P.

Barkan, L. (1975), Nature's Work of Art: The Human Body as Image of the World, New Haven & London: Yale U.P.

Barker, F. (1995), The Tremulous Private Body, Michigan: University of Michigan Press.

Barthes, R. (1990), The Pleasure of the Text, trans. R.Miller, Oxford: Blackwell.

Barton, L. (ed.), (1996), Disability and Society, New York: Longman.

Baudrillard, J. (1994), The Illusion of the End, trans. C.Turner, Cambridge: Polity Press.

Benthall, J. (1976), The Body Electric: Patterns of Western Industrial Culture, London: Thames & Hudson.

Berger, J. (1972), Ways of Seeing, London & Harmondsworth: Penguin.

Breward, C. (1995), The Culture of Fashion, Manchester: Manchester U.P.

Bryson, N. (1983), Vision and Painting: The Logic of the Gaze, London: Macmillan.

Bullock, A. and Stallybrass, O. (eds.), (1990), The Fontana Dictionary of Modern Thought, London: Fontana.

Collins, J., Radner, H. and Preacher Collins, A. (eds.), (1993), Film Theory Goes to the Movies, London and New York: Routledge.

Corbin, A. (1986), The Foul and the Fragrant, London: Picador.

Crary, J. (1990), Techniques of the Observer, Cambridge, Mass.: MIT Press.

Crary, J. and Kwinter, S. (eds.), (1992), Incorporations, New York: Zone.

Debord, G. (1983), The Society of Spectacle, Detroit, Mich.: Black & Red.

Deleuze, G. Á. and Guattari, F. (1988), A Thousand Plateaus - Capitalism and Schizophrenia, trans. B.Massumi, London: Athlone Press.

Dijkstra, B. (1986), Idols of Perversity: Fantasies of Feminine Evil in Fin-de-Siecle Culture, New York and Oxford: Oxford U.P.

Druckrey, T. (ed.), (1996), Electronic Culture, New York: Aperture.

Ewing, W.A. (1994), The Body: Photoworks of the Human Form, London: Thames & Hudson.

Featherstone, M., Hepworth, M. and Turner, B. (eds.), (1991), The Body: Social Process and Cultural Theory, London: Sage.

Feher, M., Naddaff, R. and Tazi, N. (eds.), (1989), Fragments for a History of the Human Body, Part One, New York: Zone Books.

Foster, H. (ed.), (1988), Vision and Visuality, Seattle: Bay Press.

Foucault, M. (1979), Discipline and Punish, New York: Vintage.

Frayling, C. (ed.), (1992), Vampyres, London: Faber.

Freud, S. (1983), Sigmund Freud on Sexuality, Pelican Freud Library Vol. VII, Harmondsworth: Penguin.

Gordon, C. (ed.), (1988), Power/Knowledge, Brighton: Harvester Press.

Gregory, R.L. (ed.), (1987), The Oxford Companion to the Mind, Oxford and New York: Oxford U.P.

Haraway, D. (1985), 'A Manifesto for Cyborgs: Science, Technology and Socialist Feminism in the 1980s', Socialist Review, no. 80, pp.173-204.

Heidegger, M. (1962), Being and Time, trans. J.Macquarrie and E.Robinson, Oxford: Blackwell.

Helman, C. (1992), The Body of Frankenstein's Monster: Essays in Myth and Medicine, London & New York: Norton.

Hollander, A. (1978), Seeing Through Clothes, New York: Viking Penguin.

Husserl, E. (1931), Ideas - General Introduction to Pure Phenomenology, trans. W.R. Boyce Gibson, London: Allen and Unwin.

Jacobus, M., Fox Keller, E. and Shuttleworth, S. (eds.), (1990), Body/Politics, London: Routledge.

Kierkegaard, S. (1974), Fear and Trembling and The Sickness Unto Death, trans. W. Lowrie, Princeton U.P.

Lacan, J. (1977), Ecrits: A Selection, trans. A.Sheridan, London: Tavistock Publications.

Leach, E. (1972), 'Anthropological Aspects of Language: Animal Categories and Verbal Abuse', in Maranda, P. (ed.), Mythology, Harmondsworth: Penguin.

Lucie-Smith, E. (1991), Sexuality in Western Art, London: Thames & Hudson.

Merleau-Ponty, M. (1962), Phenomenology of Perception, trans. C. Smith, London: RKP.

Mulvey, L. (1984), Visual and Other Pleasures, London: Routledge.

Nead, L. (1992), The Female Nude: Art, Obscenity and Sexuality, London: Routledge.

Negroponte, N. (1995), Being Digital, New York: A.A. Knopf.

Nicholls, P. (ed.), (1978), Explorations of the Marvellous, Glasgow: Fontana/Collins.

Nietzsche, F. (1956), The Birth of Tragedy, trans. F. Golffing, New York: Doubleday.

Sartre, J.P. (1956), Being and Nothingness, trans. H.E. Barnes, New York.

Scarry, E. (1985), The Body in Pain, New York: Oxford U.P.

Schilder, P. (1935), The Image and Appearance of the Body, New York.

Springer, C. (1996), Electronic Eros, Austin: University of Texas Press.

Synnott, A. (1993), The Body Social, London and New York: Routledge.

Webb, P. (1975), The Erotic Arts, London: Secker & Warburg.

Wilson, E. (1989), Adorned in Dreams, London: Virago.

Woolley, B. (1993), Virtual Worlds, London: Penguin.

index

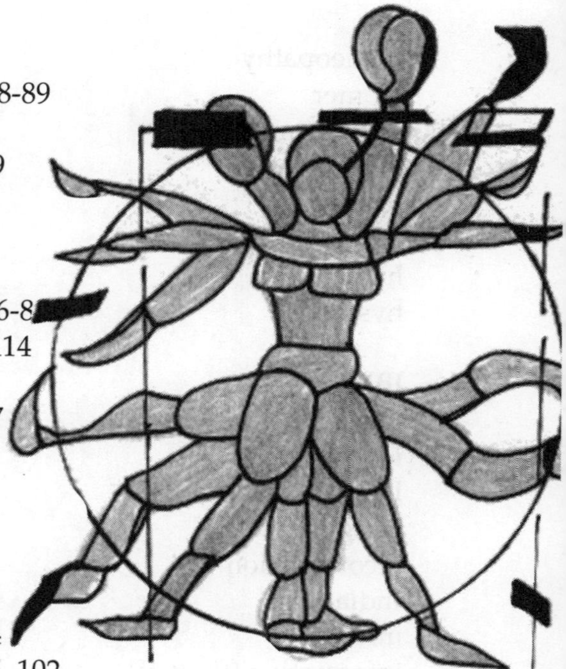

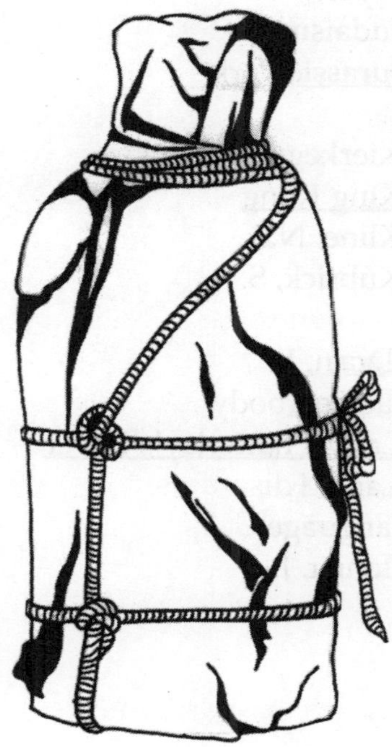

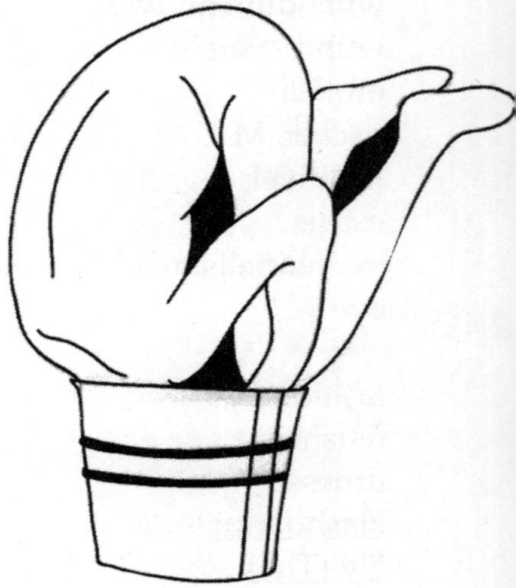

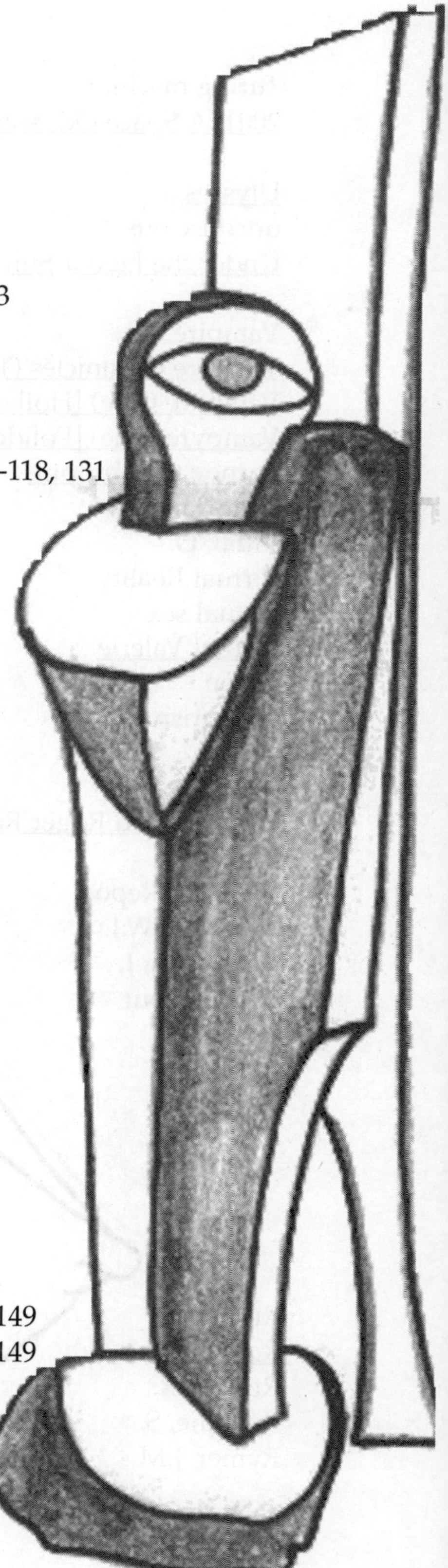

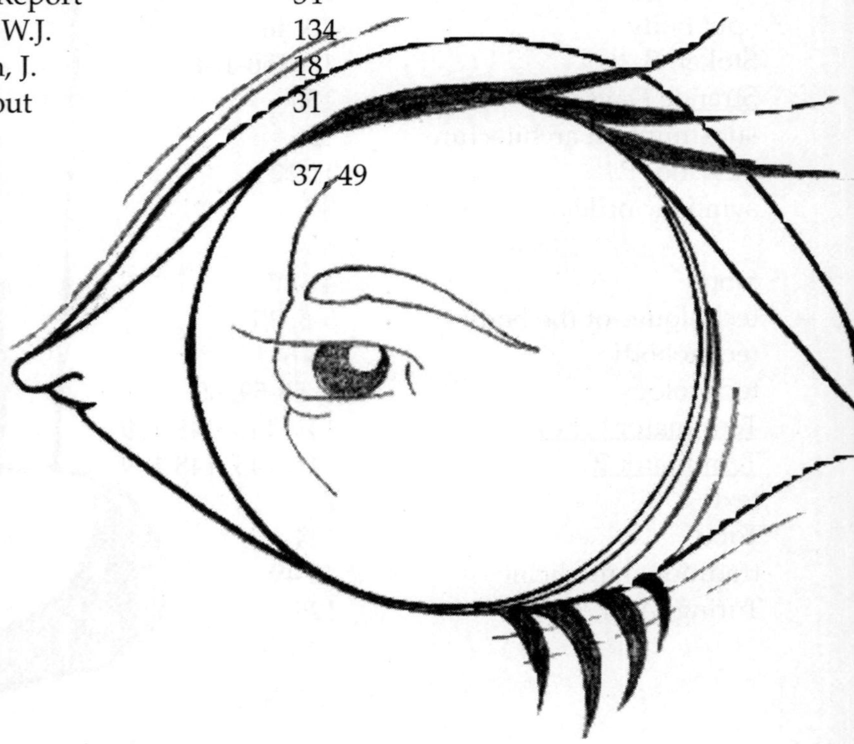